# MAKING MONEY IN MUTUAL FUNDS

**Also by Gordon Pape**

**INVESTMENT ADVICE**

Building Wealth in the '90s
Low-Risk Investing in the '90s
Retiring Wealthy
Gordon Pape's 1996 Buyer's Guide to RRSPs

**CONSUMER ADVICE**

Gordon Pape's 1996 Car Value Guide

**HUMOUR**

The $50,000 Stove Handle

**FICTION**

(With Tony Aspler)

Chain Reaction
The Scorpion Sanction
The Music Wars

**NON-FICTION**

(With Donna Gabeline and Dane Lanken)

Montreal at the Crossroads

# MAKING MONEY IN MUTUAL FUNDS

A PAPE STARTER'S GUIDE

# GORDON PAPE

PRENTICE HALL CANADA INC., SCARBOROUGH, ONTARIO

Canadian Cataloguing in Publication Data

Pape, Gordon, 1936– .
Making money in mutual funds: a Pape starter's guide

ISBN 0-13-487711-X

1. Mutual Funds - Canada. I. Title.

HG5154.5.P36 1996 332.63'27 C96-9305419

Prentice-Hall, Inc., Englewood Cliffs, New Jersey
Prentice-Hall International (UK) Limited, London
Prentice-Hall of Australia, Pty. Limited, Sydney
Prentice-Hall Hispanoamericana, S.A., Mexico City
Prentice-Hall of India Private Limited, New Delhi
Prentice-Hall of Japan, Inc., Tokyo
Simon & Schuster Asia Private Limited, Singapore
Editora Prentice-Hall do Brasil, Ltda., Rio de Janeiro

ISBN 0-13-487711-X

4 5 00 99 98

Printed and bound in Canada

Every reasonable effort has been made to obtain permissions for all articles and data used in this edition. If errors or omissions have occurred, they will be corrected in future editions provided written notification has been received by the publisher.

NAZIL

# CONTENTS

# Have a clear understanding

of what you're getting into before you invest in anything. . . . Interest in mutual funds exploded in the '90s as interest rates dropped, but many people didn't know what they were buying. . . . Doomsday predictions for the mutual fund industry have become a popular way to sell books. However, unless you expect atomic war sometime soon, ignore them. . . .

This book was written mainly for people who are dipping their toe in the mutual fund lake for the first time, although they aren't the only ones who may find it useful. Many Canadians have mutual fund investments, but are vaguely uncomfortable about the whole idea. They're into funds because they've heard about them from friends or seen them discussed in the media or read an ad or because a broker recommended them. However, although loathe to admit it, they don't really understand what they've invested in. They aren't sure whether the funds they own are the right ones, whether they've paid too much for them, how to go about judging them, when to sell them, or even what the fund portfolios hold in the way of securities. If you're in this group, *Making Money in Mutual Funds* will answer many of your questions.

Of course, if you've never bought a mutual fund in your life, a book like this is an absolute necessity. Never, never make an investment of any kind without a clear understanding of exactly what you're getting into. This is one of the cardinal rules of successful money management.

In the pages that follow, you'll find all the basics—everything you need to start to put together a lifetime mutual fund portfolio. You'll find information about the many different types of mutual funds, guidance about how to decide which funds suit your needs, details of the costs involved and how to keep them as low as possible, advice on how to pick winners, and much more.

What you won't find here are specific ratings for individual mutual funds. To go to this next stage, pick up a copy of my *Buyer's Guide to Mutual Funds*. It contains reviews and ratings for every mutual fund sold in Canada that has been around for at least three years. All the information is updated annually.

This book explains the fundamental principles of mutual fund investing—the kind of basic guidance I can no longer fit into the annual *Buyer's Guide* because the rapid growth of the fund industry has required me to devote more space to reviews and left less room for basics. (The *1996 Buyer's Guide* evaluates more than 600 specific funds.) I've tried to keep the material here as practical and non-technical as possible, while at the same time covering all the key points you should know before making an investment.

Before you become immersed in the details, a little recent history might help to put the tremendous growth of the Canadian mutual fund industry into perspective. At the beginning of the 1980s, most Canadians knew little or nothing about mutual funds. When it came to investing money, bank savings accounts were the number one choice by far. Canada Savings Bonds were also very popular. The more adventurous might have committed some cash to guaranteed investment certificates (GICs) but often with a certain trepidation.

the fine print

**DEFINITIONS AND SUCH**

You'll find this box wherever new terms or phrases are introduced that may not be familiar to most people. Also, look for more detailed explanations of technical issues here.

A national survey commissioned by the Toronto Stock Exchange in the autumn of 1983 found that only 1.5 percent of Canadians had money invested in equity (stock) mutual funds. By contrast, over 85 percent had savings accounts. As the '80s unfolded, we became a little more daring—swept along, in part, by a surging North American stock market, which enjoyed a powerful five-year run from 1982 to 1987. Canadians who knew little or nothing about stocks began to search for other ways to participate in the bonanza. Mutual funds, which were already popular in the U.S., emerged as an obvious choice.

When the TSE updated its survey in mid-1986, it found that savings accounts were as popular as ever. But the number of Canadians with money in equity mutual funds had risen to 6 percent. Then came Black Monday—October 19, 1987. The financial world watched in shock as New York's Dow Jones Industrial Average plummeted more than 500 points. It was the biggest one-day loss in history, worse even than the crash in 1929. The Toronto Stock Exchange went on the same elevator plunge. Many investors panicked, dumping their shares and equity funds for whatever price they could salvage.

It took a long time for those wounds to heal. As the 1990s began, the Investment Funds Institute of Canada—the industry association of the mutual funds business, more commonly known as IFIC—reported that the total assets under management for all member companies stood at just under $23.5 billion. Of this, less than half—$11.2 billion—was invested in funds that specialized in common stocks, either Canadian or foreign. The rest was in more conservative funds that focused on cash, bonds, mortgages, and preferred shares.

inside info

**PROFITS, PROFITS, PROFITS**

When you see a box like this, read it carefully. The specific advice it contains is designed to help you improve the returns on your mutual fund investments.

The **stock market boom of 1993** brought the Canadian mutual fund industry the biggest growth spurt in its young history.

And then, suddenly, the explosion happened. Even with Canada mired in recession, money began flowing into mutual funds in the early '90s. Assets of member companies of IFIC tripled during the period from January 1, 1990, to the end of 1992. In part, this was due to more mutual fund groups joining the umbrella organization. But much of the growth was directly attributable to rapidly declining interest rates, which pushed Canadians to start searching for other investment alternatives.

The stock market boom of 1993 brought the Canadian mutual fund industry the biggest growth spurt in its young history. In a single year, total assets under management surged from $67 billion to almost $115 billion—a one-year gain of $48 billion! The total invested in common stock funds alone rose to $50 billion—a gain of almost five-fold in four years. The pull-back in stock and bond markets in 1994 slowed the frantic growth pace, but didn't stop it. At the end of October 1995, total mutual fund assets were almost $138 billion.

Some industry-watchers are predicting a **$500-million mutual fund industry** in this country by the year 2000.

And yet, rapid as it has been, the growth we saw in the first half of the '90s may be just the beginning. Some industry-watchers are predicting a $500-million mutual fund industry in Canada by the turn of the century, which is just a few years away. There are several reasons for their confidence:

- The long-term trend in interest rates is down. This makes investments like GICs and Canada Savings Bonds less attractive, so people look elsewhere for higher returns. Mutual funds are an obvious choice.

- Banks have cut the interest rates paid on savings accounts to the bone. In many cases, the return may be less than 1 percent unless a substantial amount of money is held in the account. There are mutual funds that are almost as safe as bank accounts and that pay four or five times more.

- The plunge in the value of the Canadian dollar in the early '90s and concerns about Quebec separatism awakened many people to the desirability of moving some of their investments outside the country. International mutual funds provide a simple, easy way to realize this kind of financial self-preservation.

- The rapid growth of the mutual fund industry made it possible for investment companies to offer a wider range of products. As a result, the marketplace now offers something for everyone.

- Mutual fund marketing has become much more sophisticated in recent years. In the past, most funds were sold like encyclopedias, with sales reps using a hard-nosed, sign-here-and-out-the-door approach. The adage was, Mutual funds are sold, not bought. While there are still criticisms of some fund sales and advertising techniques, we've come a long way in a short period of time.

- Although billions of dollars have flowed into Canadian mutual funds in recent years, we're still far behind the

know yourself

**PERSONAL INSIGHTS**

One of the keys to successful mutual fund investing is understanding what kind of money manager you are and setting appropriate objectives. These boxes offer special insights into your own personality, which may help you achieve these goals.

Americans on a per capita basis when it comes to this type of investment. This suggests that as long as there's no repeat of the '87 crash, Canadian per capita mutual fund investments should continue to grow at a fast pace.

All this investment activity leaves many people wondering whether it is all a fad. Will the mutual fund industry come crashing down like a modern-day South Sea Bubble?

I'm asked this question at almost every investment seminar I give these days.

The quick answer is no. Now let me qualify it. The current popularity of mutual funds could be seen as an investment fad in the sense that a lot of money has been directed into one business within a relatively short period of time. But to go from there to predict the collapse of an industry, as a few doomsayers have done in an attempt to produce a bestseller, is not just irresponsible, it also betrays a fundamental misunderstanding of what mutual fund investing is all about.

In order for the mutual fund industry to collapse virtually overnight, all the stock markets in the world would have to crash, all the bond markets would have to follow suit, all currencies would have to be simultaneously devalued, the prices of all precious metals would have to tumble and all real estate values would have to plummet. Mutual funds invest in all these things and more. So for the whole industry to be wiped out, every asset in the world would have to lose substantial value. A major atomic war would produce this result. A giant meteor colliding with our planet would, as well. So would a huge solar flare that incinerated all life on Earth. I can't think of much else that would.

It's true that individual mutual funds may take a nosedive. It's also possible that all the funds within a specific group could be hit at the same time. If the American stock markets were to plunge, for example, all U.S. equity funds would go down, too. But other types of funds might well thrive in such a situation. When stock markets crashed in 1987, governments around the world immediately made big cuts in interest rates in an effort to restore confidence and increase money flows. As a result, people holding bond mutual funds instantly realized big gains. In my own case, any losses I suffered in my stock funds were more than offset by profits in my bond and mortgage funds. The point is that a well-diversified mutual fund portfolio carries its own built-in insurance against wholesale financial collapse. This book will tell you how to put together such a portfolio.

trade talk

**TALES AND TRIVIA**

The mutual fund business is full of interesting personalities, fascinating anecdotes and intriguing trivia. You don't need to read these sections to be a successful fund investor—but you'll know a lot more about the business you're entrusting with your money if you do.

So don't let the doom-and-gloomers make you uptight or dissuade you from putting some money into what I believe will be the number one choice for 21st-century investors—mutual funds! So much for the introduction. Now it's time to get down to business.

# A mutual fund is simply a

pool of money from a number of individuals that is turned over to a professional manager to invest on their behalf. . . . Mutual funds invest in a wide range of securities. Some focus exclusively on the stock market, but there are many funds that own no stocks at all. . . . A mutual fund will earn profits or suffer losses on the basis of how well the investments in the portfolio perform. . . .

What is a mutual fund? Good question. And if you don't know the answer, don't feel badly. Many other people are in the same boat, including some who own mutual fund investments. Here's how I explain the concept when I'm giving a seminar on mutual fund investing. Pretend for a moment that you're sitting in a room with 1,000 other people listening to me discuss the subject. Let's start by supposing each of you had to pay $10 to attend this seminar. That's a total of $10,000 collected at the door. Now I surprise you by saying that I'm not going to keep that money as my fee. Instead, I'm going to invest it on your behalf in Canadian stocks. In its simplest form, I'm going to create a Canadian equity mutual fund, with me as the manager and the seminar attendees as the unitholders.

Your $10 buys you one share in this new venture—there are 1,000 shares in all, one for each person at the meeting. I ask you all to reconvene at the same place in exactly one year and I'll tell you how your investment has done. This will be our annual meeting.

trade talk

## MANAGEMENT FEES

Management fees and expenses normally range from a low of 0.5 percent of a fund's total assets to a high of about 4 percent. The lower the total management expense, the more profits that are left for distribution to investors.

the fine print

## OPEN-END FUNDS

An open-end mutual fund is one in which units are bought and sold directly by the fund's treasury, on the basis of the current market value of the portfolio. In most cases, the portfolio is revalued every day. A closed-end fund is one in which no new units are made available after the initial selling period. The only way to buy or sell shares is by dealing with another investor. Units in closed-end funds usually trade on a stock exchange.

The next day, I choose some stocks for the fund and purchase them on behalf of you and the others who attended the seminar. Those stocks become the fund's investment portfolio. During the year, I buy and sell some more stocks, hopefully producing some profits along the way. For my services, I withdraw $25 from the fund's assets each month. This is my management fee. Of course, this amount seems ridiculously small. But if the fund were to grow in time to $1 million, the fee would increase 100 times to $2,500 a month. When you consider that a number of mutual funds in this country have assets in excess of $1 billion, you begin to appreciate the profit potential for good money managers. The fund also incurs some other expenses, such as brokerage commissions for the shares purchased. These costs are paid with the cash remaining in the fund.

At the end of the year, we reconvene and I tell you what has happened during the past 12 months. If the news is good and your original $10 stake is now worth $15, I might ask for a performance bonus. Since you'd all be feeling pretty happy about a 50 percent increase in your money, you'd presumably vote to grant it.

But suppose the news was bad. It turned out that I was a lousy money manager and your original $10 was now worth only $5. Chances are your immediate reaction would be to get out—to sell your unit, even if it meant locking in the loss of half your stake. If this were a true, open-end fund, the only way to do this would be to have me redeem the unit and pay you the cash from the fund's assets. You couldn't sell your share directly to another investor.

If you decided to hang in, despite the rotten results, your alternative might be to demand that I quit as manager. You might say to me, "Get someone else who can invest the money more effectively or we'll all pull out our cash." This rarely happens in the real world, but it's possible if unitholders get angry enough. In any event, you wouldn't have to vote on a motion to grant a performance bonus. I'd be fighting just to keep my job.

the fine print
**THE PROSPECTUS**

A simplified prospectus is a document that summarizes all the terms and conditions governing a specific mutual fund or group of funds. Salespeople are required by law to provide you with this document before finalizing an order. While no one ever reads these things from cover to cover, there are some key points you should routinely check out. See chapter 8 on for details.

There are **more than 1,000 mutual funds** in Canada and the number is increasing every year.

There, in a microcosm, is the world of mutual funds. A fund is simply a pool of money put up by a number of individuals and handed over to a professional money manager to invest on their behalf. Certain criteria will govern the operation of the fund—what it can invest in, what fees it can charge, what kinds of risks it can take. These will be

spelled out in detail in a *simplified prospectus*—a document you must be provided with before any order can be finalized.

Mutual funds come in a great variety of shapes and sizes. Some funds may have only a few hundred thousand dollars in assets; others are worth more than $3 billion.

There are more than 1,000 mutual funds in Canada now and the number is increasing every year, which is both a curse and a blessing. The curse is the confusion created by such a huge choice of investment options. With so many funds from which to select, some people are unable to make up their minds about which way to go. The blessing comes from the fact that this wide choice translates into greater profit potential and reduced risk. In the old days, there were few safe havens to turn to when the investment seas became rough. Today there are many funds that offer calm waters in which to ride out the storms that occasionally hit the real estate, stock, and bond markets.

Choosing the right funds from this rapidly expanding universe isn't easy and will become more difficult in the future as even more new entries appear. But it's well worth making the effort, for reasons I'll explain in the next chapter.

# Mutual funds give you

the services of high-priced money managers at bargain basement prices. You can spend $60,000 to build a well-diversified portfolio or you can do it with a fund for as little as $500. . . . Funds are now the most convenient type of investment you can make—they're available on almost any street corner. . . .

I've heard all kinds of excuses for not investing in mutual funds: "They're too risky." "I don't understand them." "They're too expensive." "I tried it once and lost money." "The salespeople use too much pressure." "They're a fad." In specific cases, each of these protests could be valid. It's certainly true that some funds are high risk, that some cost too much, and that some have a flavour-of-the-month aura. But to focus too narrowly on the flaws in mutual funds is a classic example of missing the forest for the trees.

Mutual funds offer advantages that a small investor simply can't find anywhere else, which is why they've become so popular. Here are the key benefits:

### PROFESSIONAL MANAGEMENT

The people who run mutual funds are professional money managers, usually with impressive credentials and years of experience. This doesn't mean they are all good. As in any other business, you'll find some managers that are brilliant, some that are mediocre, and some that are downright inept.

The good news is that with mutual fund managers, it's somewhat easier than in most professions to sort out the wheat from the chaff. The Canadian Medical Association isn't going to tell you which doctors are great and which are incompetent, and there are no published figures on a surgeon's percentage of successful operations last year. The Canadian Bar Association doesn't publish a monthly won–lost record for trial lawyers. But mutual fund managers have the results of their labours publicly displayed all the time. When the fund statistics come out each month, you can tell at a glance who is at the head of the pack and who is trailing behind. These statistics don't tell the entire story, of course. But they provide public insights into a person's ability that few other professions outside of pro sports offer or would even tolerate.

## Mutual funds provide the opportunity to obtain professional management even though you may have only a few hundred dollars available.

The investment world has become immensely complex over the past 20 years. Very few people have the time, knowledge, or inclination to build and manage a diverse portfolio of stocks, bonds, cash, and real estate. As a result, money management has become a large and growing business. But hiring your own money manager can be very expensive. Usually, a professional won't even consider taking you on as a client unless you have at least $100,000 to invest; others won't consider less than $1 million. If you do have this kind of money, the fees can be expensive—usually 1 to 2 percent of your total assets under management.

Mutual funds provide the opportunity to obtain professional management even though you may have only a few hundred dollars available. In percentage terms, the price may be higher than you'd pay for individual attention. But the actual dollar amount will be low, because most people don't have big bucks to invest. If you put $1,000 into a fund that has a management expense ratio of 2.5 percent, your actual annual charge for professional money management will only be $25. If you think you can do better and save this fee, go to it. You don't need this book.

## PORTFOLIO DIVERSIFICATION

One of the main problems faced by small investors is that they don't have enough money to properly diversify their holdings. To put together a well-constructed stock portfolio, for example, you'd need to hold shares in about 16 companies. Properly chosen, this would give you a position across about 80 percent of industry groups.

### the fine print
### RATIO RATIONALE

The management expense ratio (MER) is calculated by adding up all management fees and other expenses (such as brokerage commissions) that are charged to a fund and dividing this amount by the fund's total assets. Thus a fund with total expenses of $250,000 and assets of $10 million has an MER of 2.5 percent.

To buy a board lot (100 shares) of each at an average price of $20 a share would require an outlay of $32,000. But this would only give you a basic stock portfolio. For proper balance, you'd need to add some fixed income securities, such as bonds, and some money market funds to your mix. Total cost for a well-diversified plan: say, $60,000.

So, what's so important about diversification? you may ask. Risk reduction, that's what. Professional money managers have two main goals. One is to achieve above-average returns. The other is to ensure that in the event that something goes wrong their clients aren't hit any harder than necessary.

This is where diversification comes in. If you invest all your money in one stock and the company goes under, you've lost 100 percent of your assets. If you invest equally

**DISCIPLINARY ACTION**

Some of the most successful mutual funds in Canada place strict limits on the size of their portfolios. Trimark, for example, limits its equity funds to about 50 stocks. If the managers want to add a new one, they have to show why it's a better fit than a security already in the fund, because something has to go to make room. This brings a high degree of discipline to mutual fund management, which often pays off in better returns for investors.

in two stocks and one collapses, you've lost 50 percent. If you spread the same amount among four stocks, you've lost 25 percent of your money. At 10 stocks, your loss drops to 10 percent. At 20 stocks, 5 percent. This is the advantage of diversifying. By spreading your risk, you limit the damage if one security goes south.

Mutual funds, of course, do all this for you. When you buy units in a mutual fund, you're buying a share in the fund's investment portfolio. If you want to know exactly what this consists of, ask for a copy of the fund's latest financial statements. They'll tell you what assets the fund was holding as of the record date.

In some cases, there may be hundreds of individual securities within a portfolio. This degree of diversification isn't necessarily a good sign; the more securities a fund owns, the more difficult it is for the manager and staff to keep on top of everything. Ideally, I prefer to see a portfolio of 25 to 50 securities. It gives me a higher degree of confidence that the manager has the fund's investment policy under control and is able to carefully monitor everything in the portfolio on a day-to-day basis.

## VARIETY

Only a few years ago, the mutual fund marketplace in Canada was very limited. But now there's a vast array of products on the shelf. At the beginning of 1996, more than 1,000 mutual funds were on offer, and the number continues to grow. This growth has been good news for investors on several counts.

In the late '80s, there were few books about mutual funds and the business media virtually ignored the topic. Now the press carries daily reports on the industry and mutual fund managers have become media stars.

First, more funds mean more choice. The chance of finding a fund that exactly matches your requirements is improved. As well, the range of investment options offered by funds has expanded. At the beginning of the '90s, funds specializing in emerging markets, high yield bonds, telecommunications, health sciences, Latin America, and technology were unknown in this country. Now all these choices, and others, are available.

Furthermore, increased competition leads directly to better service and lower fees. When a few fund companies dominated the market, they could more or less call the shots. This is no longer possible. One example of the benefits of a more competitive environment: the day of the mandatory 9 percent front-end load is long gone.

Finally, a larger industry means much more analysis and information. When I first started to write about mutual funds in the late '80s, there

trade talk

**HIGH-FLYERS**

Some of the new types of mutual funds have been among the hottest performers. In 1994, for example, the Regent Korea Fund, a specialized international fund that didn't even exist when the decade began, turned in the best result in the country, with a gain of 31.1 percent. The runner-up, in its first full year of existence, was the Green Line Science and Technology Fund at 28.3 percent. Started in late '93, it was the first Canadian mutual fund to focus exclusively on the fast-growing technology sector.

were few books on the subject and the business media virtually ignored the topic. Now the press carries daily reports on the industry and mutual fund managers have become media stars; there are several newsletters devoted exclusively to fund investing strategies and, at last count, there were five annual consumer guides being published about mutual funds. There's no longer any reason to remain ignorant about mutual fund investing!

### CONVENIENCE

Perhaps the biggest advantage mutual funds offer is convenience. They're available at almost every corner. Walk into any branch of any bank or trust company and you can invest in mutual funds. You can pick up the phone and build a portfolio from your home. You can order funds by mail. You can buy them on the Internet. If you wish, some fund salespeople will even come to your home to take your order. No other form of investment has made itself so readily available to the ordinary investor. You need a broker to buy stocks or bonds. Investing in real estate is an immensely complicated procedure. Even GICs and Canada Savings Bonds aren't as ubiquitous.

trade talk

**HOT LINES**

Some mutual funds are sold almost exclusively over the phone, but you have to call these companies—they won't solicit you. Two examples are the highly successful Altamira funds, which pioneered funds-by-phone in Canada, and the U.S.-based Scudder funds, which invaded the Canadian market in late '95.

### PROFITABILITY

There's no guarantee that any given mutual fund will make money, of course. But, if you hold onto it long enough, the odds are that it will end up in the black. During the decade ending October 31, 1995, only one of the myriad funds in existence reported a negative return. All the others made money, even though this period included the stock market crash of 1987.

Of course, in some cases the return was less than you would have earned if you had put your money in CSBs (8.3 percent a year on average over the decade). But in most cases, the funds did much better. The average international stock fund returned 10.5 percent a year during that period, according to figures published by *The Globe and Mail.* The average U.S. equity fund spun average annual profits of 12 percent. For more conservative investors, the average Canadian bond fund returned 10.1 percent a year. Ultra-conservative mortgage funds averaged 9.3 percent—a full point better than CSBs.

So why invest in mutual funds? In a nutshell, to make money and reduce risk. Do you need any other reasons?

inside info

## THE IMPORTANCE OF ONE PERCENTAGE POINT

A mere one percentage point can add up to a significant amount of money over time. If you were to invest $1,000 a year in a mutual fund for your RRSP each year for 30 years, earning an average of 8 percent annually, your plan would grow to just over $113,000. But if the fund returned an average of 9 percent, you'd have more than $136,000 in your retirement plan, a gain of more than $20,000!

# There are three main

categories of mutual funds: cash, fixed income, and
growth. . . . Cash funds offer the lowest risk but the lowest
return, as well. . . . Bond funds aren't as safe as many
people think. However, they can produce above-average
profits under the right conditions. . . . Growth funds offer
the biggest gains, but be prepared to take more chances.

Recently, a woman came up to me after a seminar and asked if it was
"too late" for her to start investing in mutual funds. She was 70 years
old, she explained, and wondered whether funds were too risky for
her at this age. Her question reflects one of the most common mis-
conceptions about mutual funds, which is the tendency to assume that
mutual funds and the stock market are one and the same thing. I can't
tell you how many times I've heard people say they won't invest in
mutual funds because they're nervous about stocks.

Well, if this is all that's holding you back, let me lay this false im-
pression to rest once and for all. There *are* funds that invest in stocks,
of course—lots of them. But there are also funds that invest in things
that have nothing whatsoever to do with the stock market: mortgages,
bonds, Treasury bills, real estate, commodities, index futures, gold,
and a whole host of other securities. If it's a legitimate investment,
you'll probably find a mutual fund that specializes in it.

So fear of the stock market is not a good reason to pass up mutual
funds. In fact, a fund may be an excellent option for you in this situation. But you need to know which type of fund is right. The lady who

**U.S. money market funds** are best suited for those looking for a safe hedge against a drop in the Canadian dollar or for those who require frequent access to U.S. cash.

the fine print

**CASH FUNDS**

Cash-type funds specialize in short-term investments that are easily convertible to cash. They are the safest funds available because their assets are of the highest quality and lowest risk. When interest rates are low, as they were in 1993, yields on these funds are unattractive, except when they're used as an alternative to a savings account. When rates are rising, as they were in the first half of 1994, they're more attractive. Cash-type funds may also be useful as temporary parking places for money during turbulent economic times. They should not, however, be considered long-term investments.

asked if she was too old to buy funds was obviously not a candidate for high-risk ventures. However, there are plenty of conservative, income-generating funds that would be ideal for her needs—some of which have never had a losing year since they were launched.

So let's take a look at the various groups and sub-groups of mutual funds currently being offered in Canada. You can then decide which ones are right for you.

**CASH-TYPE FUNDS**

MONEY MARKET FUNDS (CANADIAN)

These invest in a variety of short-term securities including federal and provincial Treasury bills, certificates of deposit, short-term corporate notes, bankers' acceptances, and term deposits. A few offer limited chequing privileges. The unit value of these funds is fixed, usually at $10.

MONEY MARKET FUNDS (U.S.)

As the name indicates, these invest in short-term U.S. dollar securities, such as federal Treasury bills. The rate of return will usually be lower than that paid on Canadian money market funds because of the interest rate differential between the two countries. These funds are best suited for those looking for a safe hedge against a drop in the Canadian dollar or for those who require frequent access to U.S. cash.

## T-BILL FUNDS

These are similar to money market funds, but hold only government Treasury bills. This gives them added safety, but the return is usually a bit less than from standard money market funds.

### INTERNATIONAL MONEY MARKET FUNDS

The weakness of the Canadian dollar in the early to mid-'90s created a demand for money market funds that provided some currency protection but offered the potential for higher returns than U.S. dollar funds. International money market funds were the answer. These invest in short-term securities denominated in a range of currencies. Unlike other money funds, the unit value is not fixed, so these funds are subject to bigger gains and losses than other choices in this group.

### PREMIUM MONEY MARKET FUNDS

Some companies, such as the Bank of Commerce, offer special money market funds for those with a lot of cash to invest (the minimum entry fee may be as high as $250,000). The attraction is a lower management fee, which translates into higher returns.

danger zone

**A ROSE MAY NOT BE A ROSE**

Don't rely on a fund's name to tell you what it invests in. Some T-bill funds hold other assets besides Treasury bills, while some supposedly more broadly based money market funds invest exclusively in Government of Canada Treasury bills. Ask to see a summary of the fund's portfolio before putting in your money.

## MORTGAGE FUNDS

Fixed income funds specialize in investments that pay a fixed rate of return, such as bonds and mortgages. Funds like these are best suited for conservative investors wishing to minimize risk and for people who require regular income, such as retirees. These specialize in residential first mortgages, although they may hold other assets as well, such as short-term bonds or commercial mortgages. These are the lowest-risk type of fixed income fund you can buy. The mortgages held in the portfolio will normally all mature within five years. This makes them less vulnerable to loss when interest rates rise (the longer the term of a fixed income security, the more its price will be affected by interest rate movements). Mortgage funds are best suited for conservative investors looking for slightly higher returns than GICs offer. Profits are usually in the form of interest income; capital gains potential is low.

## CANADIAN BOND FUNDS

These invest in bonds issued by various levels of government, Crown corporations, municipalities, or major companies. They present a somewhat higher risk than mortgage funds because the bonds in the portfolio will usually take longer to mature than mortgages will. However, the higher risk is offset by higher returns—bond funds can be expected to generate 1 to 2 percent more each

trade talk

**FOR HIGH-ROLLERS ONLY**

CIBC's regular Canadian T-Bill Fund, which requires an initial investment of $5,000, carries a management expense ratio of 1.19 percent. Return for the year ending November 30, 1995, was 5.9 percent. But this bank's Premium T-Bill Fund, which won't consider accepting your money unless there's at least a quarter of a million dollars on the table, had an expense ratio of only 0.56 percent and a one-year return of 6.5 percent for the same period. The difference in return was almost entirely due to the management fee. It takes money to make money!

year. For example, over the five-year period ending November 30, 1995, the average Canadian mortgage fund had an annual return of 9 percent, according to figures published by *The Globe and Mail*, while the average Canadian bond fund produced 10.8 percent. Bond funds generate interest income, but also have the potential to produce big capital gains if interest rates drop dramatically, as they did in the recession of the early '90s. Don't be too quick to rush into bond funds at the first hint of a recession. Make sure there's a genuine downward trend in interest rates (not just a blip) before you commit your money. For example, the last major recession began in April 1990. But the big gains in the bond market didn't come until 1991, by which time it was clear where we were headed. And it wasn't a one-shot wonder. Bond funds continued to return solid profits through 1992 and 1993. So there was lots of time to cash in. Other Canadians can only look on with envy.

## SHORT-TERM BOND FUNDS

These are relatively new and represent a cross between a regular bond fund and a money market fund. The managers invest in bonds with relatively short maturity dates. In some cases, three years is the maximum allowed; other funds will hold bonds with maturities up to five years. The goal is to create a defensive portfolio that will provide higher returns than a money fund but will carry less risk than a standard bond fund. These funds will usually outperform regular bond funds when interest rates are rising but won't experience the good gains normally associated with declining rates.

## INCOME FUNDS

These invest in a variety of fixed-term securities, including bonds, mortgage-backed securities, and residential first mortgages. So they offer a more diversified portfolio for an income investor.

### DIVIDEND FUNDS

These invest in shares that pay a high dividend yield, thus allowing investors to benefit from the dividend tax credit. They're best suited for conservative investors in high tax brackets who want to improve their after-tax returns. In the past, the portfolios consisted mainly of preferred shares, but now some of the funds concentrate on high-yielding common stocks, such as the utilities and banks. Most of these funds are relatively safe, but their growth potential is limited, which is why they're included in this category.

### INTERNATIONAL BOND FUNDS

These have become increasingly popular in recent years. They invest in international fixed income securities, usually bonds. Some funds specialize in bonds issued by foreign governments and corporations. Others invest in Canadian bond issues denominated in foreign currencies (U.S. dollars, yen, sterling, marks), which makes them fully eligible for RRSPs. These funds are especially attractive during periods when the Canadian dollar is falling because of the profit potential from the fluctuations in currency exchange rates. For example, a bond denominated in U.S. dollars will be more valuable to a Canadian investor when our dollar is worth US75¢ than it would be with a US80¢ dollar. International bond funds are somewhat higher risk than Canadian bond funds because of currency movements as well as interest rate exposure.

**danger zone**

**TAX CREDIT LOSS**

As a general rule, don't hold dividend funds in registered plans, such as RRSPs, because the benefit of the dividend tax credit will be lost.

### CONVERTIBLE FUNDS

These specialize in fixed income securities, usually bonds or preferred shares, that can be converted into common stock at the owner's option. This allows for a steady income flow through either interest or dividends, while keeping open the possibility of significant capital gains if the price of the underlying common stock rises. These funds are rare and may be difficult to find because the supply of convertible securities has dried up in recent years.

## GROWTH FUNDS

### CANADIAN EQUITY FUNDS

These specialize in publicly traded shares of Canadian companies, although most contain some foreign stocks, as well, within the foreign content limit. The degree of risk will depend on a fund's objectives: some emphasize security of capital by investing mainly in blue chip stocks, while others concentrate on more junior issues in a relentless pursuit of big capital gains. Your choice of which funds are most appropriate should be governed by your personal financial objectives.

*danger zone*

**WATCH THOSE RATES!**

Fixed income funds react strongly to movements in interest rates. When rates fall, they'll produce better-than-average returns, as they did from 1991 to 1993 and again in 1995. But they'll lose value—sometimes very quickly—when rates rise, as they did in the first half of 1994. Bond funds are particularly hard hit in these circumstances—some bond funds dropped in value by up to 15 percent in just a few months during the late winter and early spring of '94. Panicky investors who sold watched in dismay when the bond markets rallied later in the year and in the early months of '95, more than recovering the losses.

### LABOUR-SPONSORED VENTURE CAPITAL FUNDS

These funds were created to encourage new business development in Canada by investing in small- and medium-sized companies, most of which are not publicly traded. They're high risk by nature, so governments have provided sweeteners in the form of tax credits to encourage people to take a chance.

**FOREIGN CONTENT
LOOPHOLE**

If you want to increase the
international portion of your
RRSP without running afoul of
the 20 percent foreign content
rule, choose international bond
funds that specialize in
securities that are fully eligible
for retirement plans. They're
treated as 100 percent domestic
content for RRSP purposes.

### U.S. EQUITY FUNDS

These invest mainly in American stocks. There are about 100 Canadian-based funds in this group.

### INTERNATIONAL AND GLOBAL FUNDS

These funds invest in stocks of several countries. Some limit themselves to certain geographic areas (Europe, the Pacific Rim, Latin America); others roam the world. International funds do not invest in their home country, global funds do.

### COUNTRY-SPECIFIC FUNDS

These concentrate on stocks of a specific nation. After the U.S.-based funds, Japan funds are the most common type sold in Canada.

### PRECIOUS METALS FUNDS

These invest mainly in gold, either directly by buying bullion or, more commonly, in shares of gold mining companies. Some funds also have holdings in other precious metals, such as platinum and silver. In recent years, shares in companies engaged in diamond exploration in the Northwest Territories have found their way into the portfolio of some of these funds.

### REAL ESTATE FUNDS

Here the managers specialize in commercial and industrial real estate. Profits are generated by capital gains and rental income, giving these funds a tax advantage. These funds ran into serious problems when property values in many parts of the country tumbled during the recession of the early '90s. As a result, only a handful of pure, open-end real estate funds are available today. However, there are a number of closed-end funds, known as Real Estate Investment Trusts (REITs), which trade on the Toronto Stock Exchange.

## DERIVATIVE FUNDS

A new category, these have been developed for RRSP/RRIF investors who wish to go beyond the 20 percent foreign content limit. Most of their assets are in Canadian Treasury bills, which are used as security for the purchase of index options on international bond and stock exchanges. I recommend caution in using them; most haven't been around long enough to establish a track record.

There are a number of subgroups in the growth fund category. Here are some of the most common:

**Socially responsible funds** These invest only in companies that meet certain standards of corporate ethics, such as concern for the environment.

**Index funds** Here the managers set up a portfolio that mirrors a key stock market index, such as the TSE 300. The idea is to consistently match the market's performance, something many equity funds cannot do. Most of these funds come close, but management fees make it difficult to achieve the objective.

**Protected funds** Managers of these funds use hedging techniques to protect the value of the assets in the event of a sharp market drop. These funds tend to underperform in good markets but limit losses in a downturn.

**GROWTH FUNDS**

Growth funds are designed to maximize profits through capital gains. Most invest in stocks, either Canadian, U.S., or international, although some specialize in commodities, precious metals, and real estate. Growth-oriented funds will generally be higher risk and suited to investors who are prepared to sacrifice a degree of safety for the possibility of higher returns. These funds are most appropriate for younger investors who have years to ride out any dips in the stock market.

**Sector funds** These specialize in a particular segment of the economy. Natural resource funds and energy funds are the most common types in Canada, although in recent years we've seen the appearance of sector funds that concentrate on health services, science and technology, telecommunications, and infrastructure companies.

**Value funds** These seek out stocks trading below book value—the price a company would be worth if it were broken up. The classic value manager tries to buy stocks for 50 cents on the dollar and then waits until the rest of the world recognizes the true worth of the shares. Sometimes this can take a long time.

**Balanced funds** As you explore the mutual fund world in more depth, you'll come across balanced and asset allocation funds. These can't be pigeon-holed into any specific class. As the name implies, funds of this type seek to build a balanced portfolio of cash-type investments, fixed income securities, and stocks. The objective is to achieve above-average growth while reducing risk exposure. Balanced fund managers will change the composition of their holdings, depending on economic conditions. So at one point in time, a particular balanced fund may be heavily invested in bonds, while at another time the emphasis may be on stocks. Balanced funds are popular with Canadian investors; there are about 170 from which to choose.

# Mutual funds are like

horses—both have performance charts, but past results don't guarantee a win tomorrow. . . . Trend lines will help you identify which funds are on the way up and which are on a slippery slope. . . . Some funds may produce fabulous results, but keep the Maalox handy!

With more than 1,000 mutual funds to choose from, it shouldn't come as a surprise that some are very good, some are very bad, and most fall somewhere in the middle of these two extremes. Obviously, you want only the very best ones for your portfolio. To heck with all the rest. There are just a couple of problems. For one, trying to pick the best funds isn't easy, which is why people like me write books on the subject. For another, the best funds for *you* won't be the best funds for someone else. It all depends on your personal goals. But there are some broad guidelines you can use to narrow down the field. Here they are:

## TRACK RECORD

Mutual funds are like horses in the sense that they have a performance record that anyone can look up. They're also like horses in another way: The results of last year's races are no guarantee they're going to win tomorrow. Past performance is simply an indication of form and nothing more.

But at least it's a starting point. One thing I can tell you with certainty after years of watching this business is that most funds establish a consistent pattern over time. You'll sometimes find a fund that rallies sharply after an off year or that slumps after a good one. However, it's rare to come across a fund that will suddenly do well after years of below-average results.

Once a fund has been around for a while (three years minimum) it develops a certain standard compared to others in the same category. The longer the fund has been in existence, the more well defined this standard becomes. Some show themselves to be highly volatile, with big up and down swings in unit value. Some turn out to be consistent performers, with little variation month after month. Some regularly outperform the competition. Some regularly underperform it.

Once a clear pattern is established, it is very likely to continue. Usually, only a managerial change or a change in the fund's investment mandate will break the long-term trend. Always remember that you can't take a short-term view in assessing a mutual fund's performance. This is especially true when the stock market is going through turbulent times.

Most equity funds will be negatively affected by downward moves in the market. Since performance numbers are recalculated monthly, this will be reflected in the results for all years being reported. The shorter the term you're looking at, the greater the impact of the most recent results. The converse is also true, of course: upward moves in the equity markets will give a bigger boost to short-term (six months to three years) returns than to longer terms (five and 10 years).

I'm often asked what rate of return is necessary for a mutual fund to get back to a break-even point

 danger zone

**SMALL CAN BE DECEIVING**

Be sceptical of spectacular performance results from small funds. Unusually high one-year returns should set off caution lights in your mind. There are a number of techniques managers can use to pump up the results of small funds, particularly on a short-term basis. So don't get too excited when a tiny new fund announces a big hit. Wait to see if the manager can keep up the pace for another year or two.

after a down year, taking commissions into account. Not surprisingly, a number of factors come into play. For starters, the lower the sales commission, the faster you'll recoup any losses. This is why it's often (but not always) better to choose a back-end load sales option or a no-load fund. Next, remember that equity funds don't increase by a predictable amount each year. They follow the fortunes of the stock market. History shows that if you invest in good equity funds when the market is going through a tough period, you can expect to reap excellent returns when it rebounds. Finally, mutual funds shouldn't be treated as one-shot investments, except in very special circumstances. By averaging your unit acquisitions over time, you'll smooth out some of the peaks and valleys.

You can find the performance history of every mutual fund in the country in numerous places. Most major newspapers publish monthly surveys of fund performance. Several organizations offer software that tracks fund results and allows you to compare those in which you're interested to the rest of the field. There are several annual mutual fund guides that assess comparative fund performance on a quantitative and qualitative basis. So there's no shortage of performance information. It's simply a matter of taking time to find it.

*trade talk*

## FAST COMEBACKS

An excellent example of this is the recent performance of the Industrial Equity Fund, a small cap fund operated by Mackenzie Financial Corporation. If you'd bought into the fund in early 1990, you'd have been tearing your hair out two years later. By the end of 1991, a $1,000 investment was worth just $697, after losses of 28.1 percent in '90 and another 3.1 percent in '91. But then came two strong years. The fund gained 23.7 percent in '92 and then turned in a breathtaking 72.6 percent performance in '93. By the end of that year, your original $1,000 was worth $1,488, and breaking even on your investment was the last thing on your mind.

Most major newspapers publish monthly surveys of
# mutual fund performance.

Just because a fund has a great 10-year record doesn't mean
it's still doing well. You have to look at the trend line—
how is the fund doing in comparison to others in the same
category?

Consider the following examples. In each case, we're
looking at the ranking of a Canadian equity fund compared to all others in the same category over several years.
See if you can spot the trend patterns. The figures cover
the decade to September 30, 1995, and are compiled by
the Southam Information and Technology Group.

|  | 10 YEARS (73 FUNDS) | 5 YEARS (136 FUNDS) | 3 YEARS (151 FUNDS) | 1 YEAR (202 FUNDS) |
|---|---|---|---|---|
| Fund A Rank | 3rd | 108th | 139th | 200th |
| Fund B Rank | 1st | 2nd | 1st | 1st |
| Fund C Rank | 48th | 91st | 11th | 19th |
| Fund D Rank | 69th | 113th | 122th | 147th |

The trends pop right out, don't they? Fund A is clearly in
a long, steady decline. There's nothing in its trend line to
encourage you to believe that next year it's going to finish
near the top of the charts. Fund B shows itself to be a win-
ner no matter what time frame you look at. Fund C is a case
where something positive is happening. Over the past three
years, it's been transformed from a weak performer to one
that's in the top 10 percent in its class. And finally, Fund D
is clearly a chronic "also-ran"—a fund that underperforms
the competition no matter what time frame you look at.

I didn't make up these performance numbers. These are
all real funds. Fund A is Cambridge Growth. At one time, it
was among the best in the Canadian equity category, but
it's fallen heavily recently.

Fund B is Multiple Opportunities, an aggressive fund that invests in junior companies traded on the Vancouver Stock Exchange. Its trend pattern shows that although it's high risk, the managers have a proven ability to stay on top. The Multiple Opportunities Fund is about as risky a mutual fund as you'll find. It invests in penny stocks: junior mining operations and start-up companies whose only asset may be a good idea. This kind of company goes belly-up more often than not, and yet the fund's managers have shown an amazing ability to pluck diamonds from barrels of cut glass. But you have to live in British Columbia to get in on the action. Other Canadians can only look on with envy.

Fund C is Cundill Security. This is a classic Cinderella fund. For years it was overshadowed by its much larger and more successful sister, Cundill Value Fund. But it got a new manager, Tim McElvaine, in 1992 and has since taken off. Remember what I said earlier about a managerial change being one of the few factors that can break a fund's pattern? Here's your textbook example.

Fund D is the AGF Canadian Equity Fund. AGF is a major player in the mutual fund business so this fund's consistently low trend line must be an embarrassment to them. They're trying to break the pattern in the same way the Cundill organization did—they brought in a new manager, Veronika Hirsch, in late '95, in an effort to shake this fund out of its lethargy.

trade talk

**COMPUTER ANALYSIS**

One of the most widely used software programs for tracking mutual fund performance is Southam's *Mutual Fund SourceDisk*. It enables you to compare any fund with all the others in the same category, and to search out the top performers in each group. The data is updated monthly. It's not cheap, but you can reduce the cost by taking less frequent updates (e.g., quarterly updates).

trade talk

**COLOURFUL CUNDILL**

One of Canada's most successful value investors is Peter Cundill, founder of the Vancouver-based Cundill Value Fund. He's known for his eye for value—but also for some of the off-the-wall things he sometimes does, like the lawsuit he launched against Mississippi to attempt to force the state to pay up on bonds it had defaulted on in the early 19th century. (Note to sceptical investors: he bought the bonds personally, not for any of his funds. His management style doesn't extend to such long-shot speculations. He says if he wins the suit, the profits will go to charity.)

VOLATILITY

Most Canadians are cautious by nature when it comes to their money. They don't like a lot of risk, and they don't like to own securities that bounce up and down like India rubber balls. Ulcers we don't need. This is why, top performer that it is, most people wouldn't put their money into the Multiple Opportunities Fund. Their nerves couldn't take it. Want proof? Look at the fund's year-by-year results from its first full year, 1986, to the end of 1994.

| 1986 | + 45.6% | 1991 | – 6.4% |
|------|---------|------|--------|
| 1987 | + 17.5% | 1992 | + 9.0% |
| 1988 | – 37.5% | 1993 | + 159.2% |
| 1989 | + 20.2% | 1994 | – 15.3% |
| 1990 | – 10.9% | 1995 | + 58.7% |

Be honest now. Would you have stayed in after that horrendous year in '88? Or after the back-to-back losses of '90 and '91? Or after the plunge of '94? Maybe you have nerves of steel. Most people don't.

This is why it's essential to look at volatility when you're trying to pick the best funds for your own needs. Fortunately, the information is easy to find. Most of the business papers include volatility rankings in their monthly mutual fund reports, so you can tell at a glance how much grief you're letting yourself in for.

THE ECONOMY

Some types of funds will outperform others at certain stages in the business cycle. For example, you can make good money in a recession, especially in the early stages, by putting money into bond funds. This is because the Bank of Canada usually moves aggressively to lower interest rates when the economy turns sour, in hopes of encouraging investment and consumer spending. Bond prices rise in a falling interest rate environment, so bond funds will do well.

Stock funds are normally the best performers when the economy is beginning to turn the corner into a recovery

**In 1993, stock markets soared and the average Canadian equity fund gained over 30 percent.**

phase. The typical pattern is that stock prices get beaten down to bargain basement levels during a recession, such as we saw in the early '90s. When economic conditions start to look better, cheap shares attract investor attention and the markets take off. We experienced a classic example of this phenomenon in 1993, when stock markets soared and the average Canadian equity fund gained over 30 percent.

The bottom line is that picking the winners isn't easy. But if you make the effort, many valuable clues are available to put you on the right track.

Volatility is a measure of a fund's tendency to fluctuate in value. A fund with a unit value that never changes would have zero volatility. The greater the swings, the higher the volatility rating. There are sev-

trade talk

**THE BIG MOVE**

The move by AGF to pluck Veronika Hirsch away from the Prudential Funds in late '95 was big news in the industry. Although not well known, Ms. Hirsch was a key contributor to the outstanding performance of several of the Prudential funds in the first half of the '90s. The Prudential Natural Resources Fund, which she managed for much of that period, was the top performer in its category over the five years to September 30, 1995, with an average annual gain of 22.6 percent. AGF was clearly hoping she'd bring her magic formula with her.

eral ways of measuring volatility, the most widely accepted being a mathematical calculation known as *standard deviation*. Many newspapers use a less complicated approach, however. For example, *The Globe and Mail* shows a fund's volatility on the basis of low, average, and high. The higher the volatility rating, the greater a fund's inherent risk.

# Set your investment goals

before putting any money into funds. . . . Know yourself.
Your investing personality is a key to intelligent fund
selection. . . . Younger investors should emphasize growth
funds. As you approach retirement, income and safety
should be your main priorities. . . .

Remember the 70-year-old woman I mentioned in chapter 4 who
wanted to know if it was too late to start investing in mutual funds?
Once we got into our discussion, she asked whether she should put
some of her money in Far East funds. I stood there for a moment with
my mouth open. A few minutes before, she had been questioning the
whole idea of mutual fund investing. Now she was talking about investing in one of the world's most volatile areas. Sure, the Far East is
an area with the potential for dynamic growth. But it's also a region
where stock markets can bounce up or down 30 percent or more within
a few months. Hardly a place for a 70-year-old looking for a safe investment and steady income. I told her as much.

The moral of this story is simple. Before you decide which mutual
fund to purchase, you must know exactly what your investment goals
are. There are mutual funds to suit every need—the trick is to match
up the right fund with your particular requirements.

To help you determine your personal priorities, I've developed a
self-test that identifies the type of investment personality you have.
Take a moment to complete it, before reading on.

Your personal investment goals will be influenced by several factors, including:

## know yourself

### PERSONAL INSIGHTS

Take this short self-test. It will help to clarify your investment objectives.

A = Agree    D = Disagree    C = Unsure

| | |
|---|---|
| I require regular investment income. | _____ |
| Safety of capital is essential. | _____ |
| Growth is not an important factor. | _____ |
| I am not prepared to take more risk for a higher return. | _____ |
| I don't want a manager with an aggressive style, even if he or she has a good track record. | _____ |
| I am within ten years of retirement. | _____ |
| I cannot afford to lose any money. | _____ |
| My spouse says mutual fund investing is too risky. | _____ |
| I'm using RRSP/RRIF money. | _____ |
| I'm more concerned with a comfortable lifestyle than with being rich. | _____ |

Give yourself two points for every "Agree," one point for every "Disagree" response. Any "Unsures" count as zero. The higher your point total, the more conservative you are, and the greater emphasis you should place on mutual funds that focus on steady income and protection of capital. If you scored 15 or higher, you should concentrate on T-bill funds, money market funds, mortgage funds, and bond funds.

If your score is in the 7-14 range, you appear to be willing and able to take greater risks in order to obtain better returns. In this case, you should be looking more seriously at equity funds (Canadian, U.S., and foreign) and precious metals funds.

If your score is less than 7, it's an indication you have done very little thinking about your investment objectives. You should take time to consider what you want to achieve before going any further.

### AGE

The younger you are, the more risk you can afford to take, although it's not a good idea to go overboard. If your first investments go sour, you may end up spooked for life. This is why it's a good idea to begin with a low-risk fund, such as a mortgage fund. This will allow you to gain some investing experience while keeping your money out of danger. As you develop a feel for what you're doing, you can move on to other types of funds.

### INVESTING EXPERIENCE

One of my cardinal rules for investors is never to put money in things you don't fully understand. Knowledge comes with experience, so until you gain some expertise, I suggest you set a goal of investing only in funds with policies and objectives you comprehend and agree with.

### INCOME NEEDS

If you're relying on money from your fund investments to live on, you'll want to select a fund that gives you a steady income.

### FAMILY SITUATION

The greater your family responsibilities, the less money you can afford to risk. A single person with no dependents can usually absorb investment losses more readily than a married couple with three children and a mortgage.

### RETIREMENT PLANS

The closer you are to retirement, the more conservative you should be in your investment choices. You may no longer have the time to ride out a serious downturn in the stock market or a precipitous drop in the price of real estate or gold. This doesn't mean you should abandon growth funds entirely, since you do need some protection from inflation, which is unlikely to stay low forever. But these funds should comprise a smaller portion of your portfolio.

### YOUR FINANCIAL AMBITIONS

Some people feel they absolutely must be rich, whatever the risk involved. If this describes you, an aggressive growth fund is the way to go. Others only want to enjoy a comfortable lifestyle, free from financial worries. They'll choose more conservative funds. Don't succumb to the "get-rich-quick" urge if you're investing inside an RRSP. If you take a hit, the money can't be replaced, and you can't claim a capital loss for tax purposes. Speculate outside your retirement plan.

All these factors must be taken into account when setting your mutual fund investment objectives. Only when you know exactly what you want to achieve, and why, should you move on to the next stage.

**inside info**

## LOW RISK, LOW RETURN

If you're looking for the ultimate in mutual fund safety, you can invest in a money market fund. However, returns are very low, especially during times when interest rates are down. A mortgage fund carries slightly more risk, but your profits should be much higher.

**danger zone** ⚠️

## CHECK THE CASH FLOW

Some so-called income funds only make distributions once or twice a year. If you're looking for regular income, such as a monthly cheque, ask how frequently money is paid out before you invest.

# Never pay more than

four percent as a sales commission. . . . Watch out for high management fees—they'll eat away at your returns. . . . Negotiable back-end loads can cost you a lot of money if you're not careful. . . .

Let's not kid ourselves. It's going to cost you some money to invest in mutual funds. The people who sell funds, manage the money, and put out your monthly statements don't work for nothing. They expect to be paid like everyone else. And the reality is, there's only one person who can pay them—you, the customer. So don't get hung up (as many people do) on the idea that no-load funds are free. They're not. They don't have any sales commission attached. However, you'll pay in other ways as this chapter will explain.

In fact, there are a range of charges associated with mutual funds. Some are obvious, some are not, but all will have a direct impact on the return you receive from your investment. Broadly speaking, these charges break down into three categories: management fees, sales commissions (loads), and miscellaneous costs. Here's a rundown on each group:

## MANAGEMENT FEES

This is an expense category that many beginning mutual fund investors don't even realize exists. In fact, this is the one common denominator among all mutual funds—every single one has a management fee of some kind. The size of these fees is an area that's becoming increasingly controversial.

the fine print

## MANAGEMENT FEES

Management fee is a catch-all term that may cover a variety of charges against a fund's assets. Wages and bonuses for the fund managers are paid out of these fees. The fee may also be used to cover certain administration expenses, accounting and bookkeeping costs, brokerage charges, and marketing costs, depending on the policy of the individual fund.

Management fees are the charges levied against a fund to compensate the people who call the shots. You won't see them as a separate charge on your statement, however, because they're deducted from the assets of the fund before the unit value is calculated. Thus makes them invisible—sort of like a hidden tax. But they'll cost you nonetheless.

The management fee is normally expressed as a percentage of a fund's total assets. Money market funds usually have the lowest fee; labour-sponsored venture capital funds the highest. The management fee cuts directly into your returns. Here's a simple example. Suppose you have money invested in a Canadian equity fund that returns 10 percent before any management fees are deducted. These expenses work out to 2.25 percent of the fund's assets. Once this money has been paid out, the actual return you'll see on your investment is just 7.75 percent. However, if the fee were lowered—say, to 1.5 percent—you'd be the beneficiary. Your return would jump to 8.5 percent. Some of the money that had been directed to management would now be going to the fund's investors.

This is becoming a hotly debated issue in the Canadian mutual fund business. Many critics of the industry feel the management fees charged in this country are far too high compared to the U.S. Fund managers respond that they don't benefit from the same economies of scale and so must charge more. But competition may soon force some changes that would benefit investors. American fund companies are showing more interest in Canada. For example, the big no-load Scudder group began operations in this country in late 1995. One of its major selling points: low management fees.

The growing management fee debate has been fuelled by the use of trailer fees. Many funds use money from management fees to cover the cost of trailer fees. This practice has become widespread in recent years, resulting in some funds increasing their management charges. In some cases, the percentage of fees taken out of a given fund has more than doubled. Because of this, past performance records of mutual funds that have escalated their fees must be taken with a grain of salt. The performance records published in the financial press cover years during which the management fees, in many cases, were lower. Had today's management fees applied at the time, the actual returns would be reduced.

## When you're considering a specific mutual fund, inquire about its management fees.

So when you're considering a specific mutual fund, ask about its management fees. A management fee of 2.5 percent or over for a stock fund is high. A fee of less than 1.5 percent is low. Also ask when the management fee last went up. If it was within the past two or three years, take

## the fine print

### TRAILER FEES

These are annual commissions paid to the person who handles your mutual fund account. They continue as long as you remain invested in the fund. The principle is similar to that used in the life insurance industry, where an agent or broker continues to receive an annual commission as long as your policy remains in force. The mutual fund industry claims trailer fees ensure investors receive continuing service from the sales representative; that he or she won't lose interest in you once the sale has been made. Critics contend such fees discourage sales reps from advising clients to redeem their units, even though conditions may be right to do so, thus prejudicing the objectivity of their advice. As well, trailer fees represent a drain on a fund's assets, reducing the return to investors.

this into account when considering the fund's performance record.

You will also see reference to a fund's management expense ratio in its prospectus and annual statements. This is the total of all management fees and other expenses charged to a fund, expressed as a percentage of the fund's total assets. These figures are regularly reported in *The Financial Post* and *The Globe and Mail* monthly fund performance surveys. The higher the percentage, the more the managers are taking off the top and the less there is for investors.

### SALES COMMISSIONS

These can take several forms, so be on your guard.

Front-end loads: These commissions are charged at the time you make your investment and are deducted from the amount of money you put up. The amount of the commission is normally calculated as a percentage of your investment. So if a salesperson charges a 5 percent front-end load, 95 cents out of every dollar you invest will go towards the purchase of fund units, while the other 5 cents is taken as commission.

The amount of commission charged will be determined by two factors:

1. The maximum commission structure authorized by the mutual fund company. The normal range for Canadian mutual funds has been between 2 and 9 percent, although many companies have reduced their maximum to the 5 to 6 percent range in recent years. Posted maximum rates often decline as the size of the investment increases.
2. Your negotiating skills. In most cases, the posted commission structure has the same effect as a manufacturer's suggested retail price. The rates are only guidelines; retailers may sell for less if they wish.

In the case of mutual funds, they usually do. Brokers, financial planners, and other fund sales representatives will generally charge a lower commission than the suggested rate, if you ask. You should never pay a front-end load of more than 4 percent, even if you're only investing $500. In these tough times, many brokers are paring down their commissions even further; 2 percent or 3 percent is not uncommon, even for small amounts. If the sales representative appears too greedy, take your business elsewhere. Don't base your decision purely on monetary considerations, however; if you're receiving exceptional service from a sales rep, an extra point or two of commission may be good value for the advice you get.

Green Line has a policy of acquiring no-load funds without charge for its customers, but levies a $45 fee when they're sold.

The only situation in which you won't be able to negotiate a discounted rate is if the fund is sold exclusively by a so-called captive sales force—representatives directly employed by the company. This applies to insurance company funds and to those sold by organizations such as Investors Group. Usually in these cases, the posted rate is what you can expect to pay. Sometimes the commissions are unreasonably high; however, some companies are reducing them to be more competitive.

You may also find there is little room to manoeuvre if you buy your mutual funds through a discount broker. This is because these companies have already cut their rates substantially. For example, Green Line Investor Services, the Toronto-Dominion Bank's brokerage arm, posts a rate of 2.5 percent on all purchases under $5,000. The rate drops to 2 percent when your order is between $5,000 and $25,000. Beyond this, the charge is only 1 percent. Even with these low posted rates, it never hurts to ask if you can obtain an additional discount. The worst the sales rep can do is say no.

You should also be aware that if you purchase no-load funds through a broker or financial planner, you may be asked to pay a handling fee. Some sales reps will acquire the funds for you without a charge, as a goodwill gesture. But others will want to be compensated for their time. This includes the discount brokers.

Green Line, for example, has a policy of acquiring no-load funds without charge for its customers, but levies a $45 fee when they're sold. Some other discount brokers, such as the Bank of Montreal's InvestorLine, charge a flat fee of $50 or $100 for buying no-load funds, except their house brand First Canadian funds. So there are times when no-load funds really aren't that at all.

Front-end loads will cut into the return on your invested money, sometimes significantly. The table below shows how much a $1,000 investment will be worth after five years and 10 years in three funds, each of which posts a 12 percent average annual compound rate of return. (Taxes have not been taken into account for the purpose of this illustration.)

| Load Charge | Amount Invested | Value after 5 Years | Value after 10 Years |
| --- | --- | --- | --- |
| None | $1,000 | $1,762.34 | $3,105.85 |
| 5% | 950 | 1,674.22 | 2,950.56 |
| 9% | 910 | 1,603.73 | 2,826.32 |

As you can see, the longer the time frame, the more significant the impact of the front-end load on the fund's accumulated value.

The effect of front-end load charges is not taken into account in the performance records of mutual funds published in the business press. But you should be aware of them because they may affect your decision about which fund to purchase.

A regular reader of my *Money-Letter* column, Dr. David Field-house, a mathematics professor at the University of Guelph, sent in a formula that you can use to determine the approximate real rate of return on any front-end load fund.

To show you how this formula works, let's say you paid a front-end load of 4 percent for a fund three years ago. According to the monthly mutual fund performance report published in the financial press, its average annual compound rate of return since then has been 12 percent. At first glance, you'd be tempted to say this fund has done better than a no-load fund with an 11 percent return

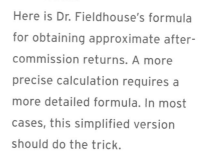

the fine print

## FRONT-END FORMULA

Here is Dr. Fieldhouse's formula for obtaining approximate after-commission returns. A more precise calculation requires a more detailed formula. In most cases, this simplified version should do the trick.

$$j = (1 + l) \times (1 - \{x/n\}) - 1$$
j = the adjusted annual rate of return
l = the published rate of return
x = the percentage of front-end load paid
n = the number of years the units are held

Note that percentages must always be expressed as decimals; for example, 8.5 percent becomes .085.

over the same period. But has it? Let's use the formula and see.

$$j = (1 + I) \times (1 - \{x/n\}) - 1$$
$$\text{Actual return} = (1 + .12) \times (1 - \{.04/3\}) - 1$$
$$\text{Actual return} = 1.12 \times (1 - .0133) - 1$$
$$\text{Actual return} = (1.12 \times .9867) - 1$$
$$\text{Actual return} = 1.105 - 1$$
$$\text{Actual return} = .105 \text{ or } 10.5\%$$

Based on true performance, once the sales charge has been taken into account, the no-load fund has a better record in this case. Keep this formula in mind when you're assessing the relative merits of load and no-load funds.

Back-end loads: Growing investor discontent with high front-end loads prompted the mutual fund industry to try a different approach in the late 1980s—the back-end load. When you purchase a back-end load fund you pay no sales commission, so all your money goes to work for you immediately. But if you redeem your fund units before a certain number of years have passed (usually five to 10), you'll be assessed a redemption fee (also known as a deferred sales charge) at this time. This fee is usually structured on a sliding scale; the longer you hold your fund units, the less you'll pay.

The back-end load has proved to be extremely popular with investors. As a result, some front-end load funds have switched to a back-end policy, while others offer clients a choice between the two options. Some major fund companies like Trimark have set up a new family of back-end load funds to meet growing customer demand.

trade talk

**REDEMPTION SCHEDULES**

The redemption fee schedule shown below applies to most Mackenzie Financial funds and is typical of this type of commission charge.

| Years Since Purchase | Redemption Fee |
| --- | --- |
| 0-2 | 5.5% |
| 3 | 4.5% |
| 4 | 4.0% |
| 5 | 3.5% |
| 6 | 2.5% |
| 7 | 1.5% |
| After 7 | 0 |

As an investor, however, you shouldn't be too quick to jump on the back-end load bandwagon. Certainly, there's no question that, all things being equal, a back-end load fund will cost you less than a front-end load fund. The problem is that things are not always equal. In fact, deciding between a front- and back-end load option has become quite difficult in some cases.

In a moment, I'll look at the cost implications of each type of fund in detail. But first, let's consider some of the disadvantages of back-end load funds.

Inflexibility Because of the way back-end loads are structured, investors are often unwilling to switch their money elsewhere, even if it makes sense to do so. A back-end load fund locks you in by setting a high premium on redemptions in the early years.

Inconsistency Back-end loads are not always calculated in the same way. You're sometimes charged on the basis of the market value of the fund at the time of redemption. However, some fund groups (Trimark and 20/20 among them) base the redemption fee on the original price you paid for the units. Find out which policy is used by the fund you're considering; all else

the fine print

## BACK-END FORMULA

Dr. Fieldhouse has also kindly provided a basic formula that can be used to determine the approximate real rate of return on back-end load funds. This is it:

$$j = (1 + I) \times (1 + q - \{p/n\}) - 1$$

All the factors are the same as before except:

p = the maximum penalty for early redemption

q = the amount by which the penalty declines annually

The formula is based on the assumption that the redemption fee will be assessed on the market value of the units when you cash them in (some funds base the charge on your original purchase cost, which is a better deal for you). A word of caution here, however: This formula only works if the redemption fee declines in equal stages over the years. If the pattern is asymmetrical (as is the case with Mackenzie, which has annual declines of 0, 0.5 percent, and 1 percent built in along the way), the formula can't be used.

being equal choose a fund that bases the redemption charge on your original investment.

Non-negotiability   Unlike front-end load charges, back-end loads are usually non-negotiable, although this is changing. Most fund companies have a fixed schedule for redemption fees, allowing you no bargaining room. However, a few have implemented flexible redemption rates, which creates a different set of problems. Inquire before you buy.

Higher management fees   Another minus to watch for is a management fee step-up. Some back-end load funds are assessed a higher management fee than their front-end brothers. The popular Trimark funds are an example. The front-end load Trimark Canadian Fund charges a management fee of 1.75 percent on the first $200 million in assets and 1.5 percent thereafter. The total management expense ratio for this fund for the year to September 30, 1995, was 1.55 percent (including GST, which must be paid on these charges against the fund). The Trimark Select Canadian Growth Fund, which can be purchased on an optional front- or back-end load basis, had a management expense ratio of 2.43 percent. The difference in the management costs of the two funds—almost 1 percent in favour of Trimark Canadian—goes right to the bottom line in calculating unit values. What it means to you is that if the two funds produced exactly the same return, the holder of units in the Trimark Select Canadian Growth Fund would end up with about 1 percent less in net yield.

Now let's take a look at how all this translates into dollars in your pocket. The results that follow may shock you, as they have many who were first exposed to them at the seminars I've given for the past few years.

We'll begin with the Trimark funds. As I've previously pointed out, those choosing the Trimark Select Canadian Growth Fund will pay a higher management fee than investors who pay a front-end load and buy units of Trimark Canadian. Which choice works out better? Take a look at the tables on the next page. In each case, I've assumed an initial investment of $10,000 and an annual rate of return for the fund of 10 percent, before management fees are deducted. For the Trimark Canadian Fund, I've assumed a front-end load of 4 percent. The back-end load shown for the Trimark Select Canadian Growth Fund for five years is 2 percent, the rate that would be applicable at the beginning of the sixth year after purchase, and is based on the initial cost of the units. For later years, the redemption fee is zero so the costs are strictly related to management fees. I've used the funds' management expense ratio as of September 30, 1995, for the purpose of this calculation. Remember, you don't pay these fees directly— they're deducted from the fund before the units are valued. But they affect your return nonetheless.

The column titled "Cost of Fees/Lost Return" shows the total impact of the various fees and sales commissions. This includes not only the amount of money you've paid but the additional income the fund would have earned had the fees not been charged. This gives you a complete picture of what these charges can add up to over time.

**trade talk**

**DOING IT ON YOUR OWN**

In case you're wondering how you can do these calculations yourself, there are several good software programs on the market. I used *Gordon Pape's Mutual Funds Analyzer,* published by Prentice Hall Canada. Another good one is *PowerMath for Funds,* produced by Speakman + Todd Publishing of Mississauga, Ontario. Programs like this help to reduce the guesswork when you are making the increasingly complex decision about whether to go front- or back-end load. They also perform several other useful functions. If you're computer-literate and serious about mutual fund investing, consider adding such a program to your tool box.

## TRIMARK CANADIAN

| Years Held | Fees Paid | Cost of Fees/ Lost Return | Net Return After Fees | End Value |
|---|---|---|---|---|
| 5 | $1,307.99 | $1,703.22 | 7.57% | $14,401.87 |
| 10 | 2,670.17 | 4,331.80 | 8.01% | 21,605.62 |
| 20 | 7,779.39 | 18,649.69 | 8.23% | 48,625.30 |

## TRIMARK SELECT CANADIAN GROWTH FUND

| Years Held | Fees Paid | Cost of Fees/ Lost Return | Net Return After Fees | End Value |
|---|---|---|---|---|
| 5 | $1,445.77 | $1,902.00 | 7.27% | $14,203.09 |
| 10 | 3,528.30 | 5,192.50 | 7.57% | 20,744.91 |
| 20 | 10,847.21 | 24,239.84 | 7.57% | 43,035.15 |

Take a close look at the numbers. They show that the longer you hold your units, the greater the financial advantage of paying a 4 percent front-end load instead of choosing the back-end load option, assuming the same return on each fund. Even if you hold the Trimark Select Canadian Growth Fund for just five years, a relatively short period by mutual fund standards, the front-end load is preferable—this despite the fact that Trimark's redemption fee is based on the initial purchase price, not the market value at the time of sale. Were the latter situation to apply, as it does with most fund companies, the difference would be even more dramatic.

While we're on the subject of back-end loads, let's look at the new breed of negotiable back-end load funds. Until recently, back-end loads were fixed by the mutual fund company; so you could look them up in the prospectus and not have to worry about whether someone else was getting a better rate. The redemption fee schedule clearly set out the amount you'd be charged if you sold your units at a given time. But in recent years, some fund companies have authorized several back-end load structures, thus making them negotiable. Their reasoning is that compensation is a matter to be dealt with between the buyer and the seller, and that the only role of the fund company is as an administrator. It all sounds quite reasonable, but it puts you at a serious disadvantage if you aren't aware of the flexible redemption schedule.

For an example of how all this works, take a look at the table of redemption fees allowed by Elliott & Page on p. 56. At the bottom of each column is the commission that the sales rep earns, depending on which schedule he or she persuades you to accept. In most cases, the seller will want to charge the maximum possible redemption rate, because this offers the highest commission payment. But buyers want the redemption schedule that gives them the best deal. The result is an adversarial relationship between you and your mutual fund sales rep—the last thing you want with someone who's advising you about how to invest your money.

So how do you get around this? Well, you could avoid the problem completely by buying a no-load fund. Or you can simply offer to split the commission down the middle—choose the redemption fee option that gives the sales rep a modest fee and gives you something better than the most costly redemption charge. Or you can stick with companies that still charge a fixed back-end load.

To protect yourself, always ask your sales rep if alternative redemption fee schedules exist, other than the one he or she is recommending. You'll also find details in the

trade talk

**HERE'S WHO'LL WHEEL AND DEAL**

Companies that offered negotiable back-end loads at the beginning of 1996 were Admax Regent, Elliott & Page, BPI, Global Strategy, and Sagit. But don't be surprised if many other fund companies adopt this option in the near future—it's a trend that seems to be spreading like wildfire. Inquire before buying.

## the fine print
## THE E&P PLAN

Here's an example of how the negotiable back-end load works. The table that follows comes from the prospectus for E&P's domestic and global mutual funds. You'll notice it gives several redemption fee schedules—you have to negotiate which one you'll pay with your sales rep.

Elliott & Page
Deferred Load Charge Schedule

| Year | I | II | III | IV | V |
|------|------|------|------|------|------|
| 1 | 6.0% | 5.0% | 4.0% | 3.0% | 2.0% |
| 2 | 5.5% | 4.5% | 3.5% | 2.5% | 1.5% |
| 3 | 5.0% | 4.0% | 3.0% | 2.0% | 1.0% |
| 4 | 4.5% | 3.5% | 2.5% | 1.5% | 1.0% |
| 5 | 4.0% | 3.0% | 2.0% | 1.0% | 1.0% |
| 6 | 3.5% | 2.5% | 1.5% | 1.0% | 1.0% |
| 7 | 0 | 0 | 0 | 0 | 0 |

Seller's Payment

| | | | | |
|------|------|------|------|------|
| 5.0% | 4.0% | 3.0% | 2.0% | 1.0% |

fund's prospectus, which you should read carefully before signing on the dotted line.

MISCELLANEOUS COSTS

There are a number of additional charges that may apply to the particular mutual fund you select. Inquire about them before making a purchase decision. The most common ones are:

Penalty fees   A few funds have adopted the unpleasant policy of locking you in for a lengthy period by imposing a hefty penalty if you sell your units before a certain time. These penalties are over and above any normal redemption fees. The 20/20 India Fund, for example, hits you with a 10 percent penalty if you sell within three years. The rationale is that the fund should be treated as a long-term investment. But this attempt to force people to stay in left a bitter taste in investors' mouths when the fund's asset value fell by almost 50 percent in the first year.

Redemption fees   You could find yourself having to pay a redemption charge even if you don't own any back-end load funds. As mentioned above, Green Line, Canada's largest discount brokerage house, charges $45 to redeem units of any no-load fund except their own. The discount brokerages of CIBC and Royal Bank have a similar policy, with a $40 charge. Also, some funds (including certain no-load funds) charge a redemption fee if you sell your units within a short time after purchase—90 days is common. The cost may be as much as 2 percent of your assets' value. If you need to cash out early for some reason, check the prospectus before you place the sell order to avoid an unwelcome surprise.

RRSP/RRIF fees   If the fund is held as a Registered Retirement Savings Plan or Registered Retirement Income Fund, a small annual trustee fee may be levied. A fee may also be charged for RRSP cancellation.

Set-up fees   You may be assessed a charge for opening an account with a company. Altamira, for example, has a one-time fee of $40 when you set up an account with them.

Switching fees   You may be permitted to switch from one fund to another within the same company, but a charge will sometimes apply. Note that some companies, including Altamira, limit the number of free switches each year. If you're dealing with a discount brokerage, you may be assessed a fee even for switches within a no-load fund group.

Systematic withdrawal charges   Some investors wish to receive regular payments from their fund. These are called systematic withdrawals. Some companies charge an annual fee for the service, others charge a fee for each payment, and a few hit you for both.

Termination or closing fees   Some plans assess a nominal fee for closing an account. This practice is becoming more widespread.

Transfer fees   This is a charge for transferring a registered account, such as an RRSP, to another financial institution or mutual fund group. It's also becoming increasingly common. Green Line charges $50 for transfers.

Withdrawal fees   A few funds charge a nominal fee for any withdrawals made from your account.

inside info

**GETTING A BETTER DEAL**

Some companies reduce or eliminate certain fees as a sales promotion tool. For instance, some fund groups have dropped trustee fees for RRSP accounts. Ask your sales representative if any deals are available.

# Reading a prospectus may

be tough, but the information it contains is critical. . . . Pay

special attention to the section at the front on costs, in

order to avoid unpleasant surprises. . . . Some fund

companies are making their prospectuses more

accessible—and your life a little easier. . . .

the fine print

**THE PROSPECTUS**

A prospectus is a legal document
that is approved by a securities
commission before it is
distributed to potential investors.
It contains details of the terms
and conditions of a securities
offer, including all the costs
involved, a summary of the risks,
and the tax implications.

Before you buy units in any mutual
fund, you should be given a copy of
something called a *simplified prospectus*. Your first reaction may be to ignore it—most prospectuses are
boring-looking documents, filled
with small print and legalese. The
best I can say about the majority of
them is that they're a great cure for
insomnia. But, even though it may
be a struggle, it's worth making an
effort to read through the prospectus
when it arrives. It contains vital information that you should be aware of before making a final decision.

Here are some of the most important things to watch for:

## INVESTMENT OBJECTIVES

This paragraph sets out the goals of the fund's managers. Sometimes
these goals can be stated in a single sentence, as in the prospectus for
the Phillips, Hager & North Canadian Equity Fund: "The principal

## the fine print

**OFFERING MEMORANDUM**
This serves the same purpose as a prospectus, but the term indicates that shares in the security are being offered only to "sophisticated" investors on a private placement basis and that a high minimum subscription will be required. The amount depends on the province where the issue is taking place and can range from a low of $25,000 to a high of $150,000. Clearly, any funds that are sold on an offering memorandum basis are intended only for the super-rich.

objective of the Canadian Equity Fund is to achieve superior results through investment primarily in Canadian equity securities." At first glance, this may not seem to say much; however, there is actually a great deal of information here. Some of the key terms:

*"Superior results"* This means the fund will seek to outperform the TSE 300 Index as well as other investment funds of the same type. The term implies an aggressive investing approach by the fund's management.

*"Equity securities"* This is a stock fund. If this troubles you, this is not your fund.

*"Primarily Canadian"* This phrase tells you that most, but not all, of the fund's holdings will be in shares of Canadian companies. However, the managers have allowed themselves some leeway to invest in international securities by inserting the word "primarily."

Contrast this statement of objectives with the one for the same company's money market fund: "The principal objective of the Canadian Money Market Fund is to achieve a high level of current income consistent with the preservation of capital by investing exclusively in short-term Canadian money market securities." In this case, the prospectus reveals that you are dealing with a fund that emphasizes yield ("high level of current income"), safety ("preservation of capital"), and short-term securities such as Treasury bills. You're told all the assets of the fund will be Canadian; there is no foreign content whatsoever. Obviously, this is a very different approach from the stock fund. Which fund you choose will depend on how your own objectives match those set out by the fund managers in the prospectus.

**the fine print**

**WHAT YOU'LL FUND**

A typical prospectus contains the following vital information about the mutual fund:

1. Investment Objectives
2. Investment Policies
3. How to Buy
4. Buying Units
5. Grandfather Privileges
6. Selling Units
7. Management Fees and Operating Expenses
8. Risk Factors

## INVESTMENT POLICIES

Some funds may have specific policies that place limits on the investments they can make to achieve their objectives. You should be aware of these policies before proceeding. For example, the simplified prospectus of the Ethical Funds family states the managers will exercise social responsibility in selecting which securities to purchase. Therefore, "the monies of the Funds will only be invested in securities of North American corporations which meet the criteria established from time to time by the Trustees." Obviously, if you don't agree with the restrictions placed on the managers, you won't invest in these funds.

The managers of the **Ethical Fund Family** exercise social responsibility in determining which securities to include in their portfolios.

## HOW TO BUY (METHOD OF SALE)

This section tells you whether the fund is open- or closed-end. If the paragraph contains a line that states the fund will sell units on a continual basis at their net asset value, it is an open-end fund. If it states that sales are to be limited in any way—either through the total number of units sold or by a time limit on sales—it is a closed-end fund.

## the fine print

### WHERE THE ETHICAL FUNDS INVEST

The prospectus for the Ethical Group of Funds lists the specific investment criteria that are applied as follows:

Ethical Growth Fund

1. The corporation must have either its registered or head office located in Canada and its shares and other securities must be either traded or about to be traded on a stock exchange in Canada.

Ethical Money Market Fund, Ethical Income Fund, Ethical North American Fund, Ethical Balanced Fund

1. The corporation must have either its registered or head office located in North America and its shares and other securities must be either traded or about to be traded in North America.

All Funds

2. The corporation should encourage progressive industrial relations with all members of its staff or employees.

3. The corporation should regularly conduct business in, and with, a country or countries that provide racial equality within its or their political boundaries.

4. The corporation should not derive a significant portion of its income from tobacco.

5. The normal business of the corporation should be the provision of products or services for civilians (non-military).

6. If the corporation is an energy corporation or utility, its major source of revenue should be from non-nuclear forms of energy.

7. The corporation should consistently strive to comply with environmental regulations established by governments and government agencies, and to be committed to implementing environmentally conscious practices.

### PURCHASING UNITS

This segment is one of the most important in the prospectus. It provides all the key information you need about the actual procedure for buying fund units, including all the costs involved. I've drawn on the simplified prospectus issued by the Pursuit Group of Mutual Funds, managed by Nigel Stephens Counsel Inc. of Toronto, for the purpose of illustration.

*How to buy*   The prospectus states orders for units may be placed through "the Manager . . . or through agents, brokers, investment dealers, securities dealers or mutual fund dealers." This tells you units in the company's funds are readily available through a variety of sources (this is not always the case) and that they can be purchased directly from the manager of the funds if you prefer not to work through a broker or agent.

*Initial investment*   The prospectus states that "the minimum amount for initial investment in each Fund is $500" before commissions. This is relatively low by mutual fund standards; many funds require at least $1,000 to open an account.

*Subsequent investments*   After you're in, the prospectus states that the minimum amount for additional investments is only $50. Again, this is low and tells you the funds are encouraging small investors.

## PROVINCIAL LIMITATIONS

Some prospectuses will state that the funds are not sold in certain provinces. This is because they have not been registered with the provincial securities commissions in those jurisdictions. In other cases, there may be no definitive statement of where the funds are available and you may have to contact the manager directly. This is the case with The Pursuit Group. The prospectus doesn't spell it out, but these funds are currently licensed only for sale in Ontario.

## LOAD CHARGES

The prospectus sets out in detail any load charges that may have to be paid. In the case of The Pursuit Group, a front-end load (called in their prospectus an "initial sales commission") may apply. Their fee scale looks like this:

| AGGREGATE PURCHASE PRICE (INCLUDING COMMISSION FEE) | MAX. SALES COMMISSION AS A PERCENTAGE OF AMOUNT PAID | MAX. SALES COMMISSION AS A PERCENTAGE OF NET AMOUNT INVESTED |
|---|---|---|
| Up to $99,999 | not to exceed 5.0% | not to exceed 5.26% |
| 100,000 to 199,999 | not to exceed 4.0% | not to exceed 4.17% |
| 200,000 to 299,999 | not to exceed 3.0% | not to exceed 3.09% |
| 300,000 to 499,999 | not to exceed 2.0% | not to exceed 2.04% |
| 500,000 or more | negotiable | |

This table contains a great deal of information. First, it tells you the company's suggested sales commissions are based on a sliding scale. The more money you invest, the lower the maximum commission will be. Second, it tells you the charges are negotiable at any level—not just in the case of the big spenders who have more than half a million to invest, even though that's the only place where the word "negotiable" actually appears. The tip-off is the phrase "not to exceed," which appears throughout. This makes it clear the percentages shown are a ceiling; sales representatives may sell for less if they wish. Third, use of the term "aggregate purchase price" means you don't have to invest the full amount at one time to get the benefit of a reduced rate. When your total holdings in funds offered by The Pursuit Group pass the $100,000 mark, your maximum commission will be reduced to the next lowest level.

Further on in this section of the prospectus, it states that any units held by a spouse or minor children can be included in calculating the aggregate amount for commission purposes.

The middle column states the maximum load charge as a percentage of the total amount you put up. The third column expresses it as a percentage of the net amount that's actually invested on your behalf after fees, and gives you a truer picture of how much sales commission you're paying. For example, if you invest $1,000 and pay a 5 percent load, it will cost you $50. This leaves $950 for the purchase of fund units. If you express that $50 commission as a percentage of $950, it works out to a load charge of 5.26 percent.

### GRANDFATHER PRIVILEGES

Some mutual funds have moved from no-load to load status in recent years. The Pursuit Group is in this category, so they offer special privileges to investors who were in their funds at the time of the change-over. This is expressed in the prospectus as follows: "Investors who were Unitholders in a Fund prior to August 21, 1987 will be entitled to purchase units through the Manager without any sales commission so long as they remain Unitholders in a Fund." However, this privilege won't be extended automatically. The prospectus states: "It is the investor's responsibility to advise the Manager or his Agent that he may be entitled to this benefit."

## REDEMPTION OF UNITS

This section of the prospectus tells you what happens when you decide to cash in your holdings. The Pursuit Group requires that your redemption order be in writing and they reserve the right to request formal confirmation of your identity (for instance, by having your signature guaranteed by a financial institution). In other words, it will take more than a simple phone call to get your money out. The prospectus goes on to state: "The redemption will be effected on the Valuation Date coinciding with or next following the date of receipt of such particulars, but no redemption proceeds will be paid until the application for redemption has been duly completed and the certificates, if any, represent-

 danger zone

## GETTING YOUR MONEY OUT FAST

If you think you might need quick access to your invested money, check out the terms of redemption carefully before buying any units. For example, all Pursuit funds except the money market fund are valued only once a week, at the close of business on Thursday. This means that if you submit a redemption request on a Friday, it could take up to two weeks to get your money (five business days after the next Valuation Day, which will be the following Thursday). Look carefully for conditions of this type in a prospectus if you think you may need your money in a hurry.

ing the Units to be redeemed have been delivered, properly executed." Payment will be made "within five business days of the relevant Valuation Date."

The Pursuit prospectus warns you that if you sell your units before 90 days, you'll be hit with a charge of up to 2 percent. Many fund companies charge for early redemption, even on no-load or front-end load funds, so check for this in the prospectus.

## MANAGEMENT FEES AND OPERATING EXPENSES

This section of the prospectus tells you how much money the managers are receiving for their services and what charges will be made against the fund. This is important information because all money paid out in this way will reduce the profits to fund unitholders.

There are two parts to this equation. One is the actual fee that's paid to the management company. The other is the day-to-day operating expenses of the fund.

It's not unusual for different funds within the same group to charge different management fees. Typically, labour-sponsored funds have the highest costs because of the intensive work involved in screening through hundreds of business plans from start-up operations. Management fees for them are typically in the 4 percent range. International equity funds are next on the expense scale, usually coming in between 2.5 percent and 3 percent annually. A notch below them are U.S. and Canadian equity funds, which typically charge 2 percent to 3 percent. Fixed income funds, like bond funds, should charge 1 percent to 2 percent. Money market funds should come in at below 1 percent.

For example, let's look at the prospectus for Mackenzie Financial's Industrial Funds. You'll see there are different management fees for each fund. These are 2 percent of the net asset value in the case of the American Fund, Balanced Fund, Dividend Fund, Equity Fund, Future Fund, Growth Fund, Horizon Fund, and Pension Fund. The Industrial Bond Fund charges 1.75 percent, Industrial Income and Industrial Mortgage Securities have a 1.5 percent fee, there's a 1 percent charge for the Industrial Short-Term Fund, and a 0.5 percent fee in the case of Industrial Cash Management Fund. This is Mackenzie's cut. With expenses added in, the percentage of the assets paid out each year increases in most cases by another quarter to half a point.

The Mackenzie formula tells you several things. First, all funds are not treated equally when it comes to management fees; the charge levied against the Cash Management Fund is one-quarter of that applied to the stock funds. The prospectus tells you, although not in so many words, that the fund managers are being well paid for their services (2 percent annually is in the top range of management fees for a Canadian-run stock fund) and that your return will be affected accordingly.

The prospectus then goes on to say that "each of the Funds (other than the Industrial Cash Management Fund) is required to pay its ongoing operating expenses." This is

the fine print

**EXPENSE SUMMARY**

You'll find a summary of all management fees as well as any expenses that will be charged directly to you at the front of the prospectus. If you don't read anything else in the document, read this page.

a significant point for you, the investor. It means the assets of your fund are not only used to pay management fees, but also must defray the cost of such things as legal charges, audit costs, custodial and safekeeping fees, taxes, brokerage commissions, interest, operating and administrative costs, costs relating to the issue and redemption of securities and costs of financial reports and other reports and prospectuses.

Policies relating to expenses vary from one fund to another. In some cases, the management company absorbs some of the charges out of its fee. In the case of these Mackenzie funds, the prospectus tells you that only the cost of advertising and dealer compensation programs will be paid by the manager; all other expenses are paid by the fund itself. Since these costs will reduce profits, the net asset value of your units will be affected accordingly.

## Most prospectuses contain a section that outlines the risk factors associated with the fund.

### RISK FACTORS

You'll find a section in most prospectuses outlining the risk factors associated with the fund. Look them over carefully and decide if they're acceptable to you. Certain types of funds will have different risk factors than others. For example, the prospectus of the Cundill Value Fund, which invests internationally, warns that "the risk of loss on foreign investments may be increased due to fluctuations in foreign currency exchange rates, less available information regarding foreign issuers, lower trading volumes, less liquid and more volatile foreign stock markets, or diplomatic developments which could affect the value of the foreign investments." In other words, the manager is warning you that there may be potential pitfalls in investing abroad and you should be aware of them before plunging in.

The AGF Group issues a different type of risk warning to those considering investing in the AGF Canadian

Resources Fund: "Investment in shares of the Fund is subject to the risks inherent in the nature of, and concentration of, investments in companies engaged in the natural resources industries. The market values of such investments and, consequently, the net asset value of the shares of the Fund, will fluctuate with, among other factors, changes in the price of natural gas, crude oil and metals caused by such factors as international monetary and political considerations, economic growth rates, trade imbalances, trade and currency restrictions between countries, government controls and conditions of scarcity or surplus." All this simply means is that if you don't like the prospects for the mining and petroleum industries, you'd better put your money elsewhere.

## TRANSFER PRIVILEGES (EXCHANGE OF SECURITIES)

This section of the prospectus tells you what rights you have if you want to switch part or all of your money to other funds within the same group. For example, anyone considering investing in Mackenzie's funds will read in the prospectus that they may be assessed a fee of up to 2 percent if they decide to move some assets from one fund to another. The good news is that if you bought the units on a back-end load basis (Mackenzie calls them "Redemption Charge Securities"), you won't trigger a redemption fee as long as the new units are acquired on the same basis.

But the prospectus warns against exchanging back-end load units for front-end units, although you have to wade through some heavy language to discover this fact: "The exchange may be subject to the applicable redemption charge based upon the issue date of the Redemption Charge Securities being redeemed and also may be subject to an exchange charge of up to 2 percent of the amount being reinvested at the discretion of your dealer. For this reason, it is generally recommended that Redemption Charge Securities should not be exchanged for Sales Charge Securities." Whew!

## READING BETWEEN THE LINES

The language on the subject of switches contained in the Mackenzie prospectus is fairly common. When you see it, be alert to the fact that there may be a financial penalty if you want to switch your money from one type of fund to another. However, it's a negotiable fee and your dealer can waive it if he or she wants to.

TAX IMPLICATIONS

The prospectus will contain one or more sections dealing with tax matters. Some of the key points to look for here are:

RRSP/RRIF eligibility  The prospectus should clearly state if the fund is eligible for inclusion in retirement savings plans, either without restriction or under the foreign property limitations. If the latter is the case, total foreign holdings in a plan may not exceed 20 percent of book value.

Taxation of dividends and interest  Payments from mutual funds are taxed differently, depending on their source. The prospectus should outline which types of payments can be expected from the fund you're considering. There are several possibilities: capital gains dividends, Canadian stock dividends, foreign stock dividends, rental income, and straight interest. You should understand what types of income you can expect to receive and determine whether this makes the best sense for you from a tax point of view. For example, if you want to shelter the maximum possible amount from taxes, you may look for funds that will generate capital gains and Canadian dividends as opposed to interest. Once you've invested, the fund manager should issue a detailed T3 or T5 slip, showing exactly how much of each type of income you receive each year.

Redemption of units  When you sell fund units, you may be subject to capital gains tax or allowed to claim a capital loss, depending on how well the investment performed. The prospectus may explain in general terms how your gains or losses are to be calculated.

## FINANCIAL STATEMENTS

The prospectus may contain the most recent financial statements of the fund. If not, it should be accompanied by a current financial report. Look over these statements, paying special attention to the following:

List of investments  The holdings of the fund as of the statement date will be shown in detail. Look down the list and see if you're comfortable putting your money in a fund with this particular securities portfolio.

Distribution of assets  The financial statements will indicate how the fund's holdings are distributed among various asset groups. See what the breakdown is among common stocks, preferred shares, bonds, mortgages, short-term notes, mortgage-backed securities, etc. You may be surprised by what you find; for example, the Industrial Mortgage Securities Fund, which may appear at first glance to be strictly a fixed income fund specializing in mortgage-backed securities, may in fact have a significant percentage of its portfolio invested in common stocks. Therefore, if you don't like the stock market, this may not be the right fund for you. So don't be guided by the name alone. See what the fund actually invests in.

Net assets  These figures will give you an idea of the size of the fund—anything over $250 million is considered large in Canada; under $10 million is small. You will also be able to see whether the fund is growing or shrinking. The latter could be a danger sign as it indicates either losses on investments or high redemptions, which could force the sale of some of the fund's securities to raise cash.

Distributions  The financial statements should show any distributions to investors and indicate what type they are (capital gains, interest, rental income, etc.). They may also provide a history of distributions over the past few years.

Management fees and management expense ratio  These should be shown in the financial statements. If some historical comparisons are included, this will enable you to see if costs have been fairly consistent over several years or have recently escalated. Look for a table like the following one, from the annual financial statements of the Phillips, Hager & North funds. This table shows the management fees and expenses of the U.S. Equity Fund.

| Year | Average Net Asset Value | Management Expense Ratio |
|------|------|------|
| 1994 | $223,908,000 | 1.07% |
| 1993 | 202,404,000 | 1.13% |
| 1992 | 155,044,626 | 1.14% |
| 1991 | 87,788,153 | 1.24% |
| 1990 | 45,568,397 | 1.21% |

As you can see, this fund's expenses have remained very consistent in relation to total assets over a five-year period, and, in fact, actually declined between 1992 and 1994. This tells you that there has been no dramatic escalation in costs or management fees recently.

Although most mutual fund prospectuses are difficult to get through, the information they contain is important and worth your time. Plus there's good news. Some fund companies are making a determined effort to lighten up their prospectuses to make them more accessible to the casual investor. Altamira, CIBC, and Hongkong Bank are three companies that have come out with user-friendly prospectuses recently. So take heart. Your life may be about to get a little easier.

inside info

**KEEPING FEES DOWN**

Phillips, Hager & North is one of the lowest-cost fund managers in Canada, which is one of the reasons its funds consistently produce above-average returns. Some other fund groups with low fees are Beutel Goodman, Bissett, Mawer, Scudder, and the MD funds (the latter are open only to the medical profession).

# The manager is the key to

a mutual fund's success. . . . It's easy to find information about fund managers, if you take the time to look. . . . Don't be too quick to follow a manager who leaves a fund—wait six months and review the situation. . . .

A mutual fund may seem rather impersonal, but it's not. Somewhere, behind the scenes, people are making decisions every day about which securities to buy, which ones to sell, what companies look promising, how much cash the fund needs, and more. They're at a computer, on the telephone, meeting with business owners, or even travelling the world in search of bargains. They're the fund managers, and they're the key to any fund's success. A good manager will consistently generate above-average returns for investors; a mediocre or poor manager will produce indifferent results.

There are a few well-known fund managers in Canada, although most toil in relative anonymity. But just because a manager isn't well known doesn't mean he or she isn't brilliant; it may simply be that the business press hasn't discovered this manager yet.

Some funds are effectively run by committee. While one person may be listed as the fund manager, decisions are really made by a group.

You may find a few companies that refuse, for reasons of their own, to disclose the name of a fund's manager, preferring to give only the name of the management company. In this case you're operating in the dark about who actually runs the fund. Thankfully, this practice is becoming rare as investors increasingly demand to know more about the credentials of the people to whom they're entrusting their money.

the fine print

## THE MANAGER

The manager decides which securities the fund will buy and sell and what the portfolio composition should be at any given time. He or she is responsible for ensuring that investment strategies are consistent with the stated objectives of the fund, for maintaining adequate cash reserves to meet redemption requests, and for complying with the regulations for mutual fund investing laid down by various securities commissions and other regulatory bodies. The manager's success or failure in making these decisions will determine how well a fund performs. The better the performance, the more investors the fund will attract and the more profitable it will be for the mutual fund company. So fund managers have an extremely heavy burden on their shoulders—and the best are very well paid for their services.

A few funds actually bear a manager's name, although in some cases the responsibilities may have changed over the years. For example, Sir John Templeton remains the guiding genius behind the Templeton family of funds, but he doesn't actively run the funds anymore. He lives in semi-retirement in Nassau, appearing at the company's annual meetings and freely giving interviews to business journalists who want to know the secrets of his success. But the actual decision-making is in the hands of a new generation of fund managers, who are well steeped in Sir John's value investing approach.

At the beginning of the '90s, most Canadian investors probably couldn't name a single mutual fund manager other than, perhaps, Sir John. But that has changed as mutual funds have caught the public's attention in recent years. Many fund managers are now regularly quoted in the business press, are seen in TV ads, and hold very well attended seminars. Frank Mersch of Altamira and Kiki Delaney of Spectrum United are just two of the managers who have captured investor interest.

Most managers aren't as well known, of course. But many have well-established credentials and a solid track record. For example, few investors know the name of Larry Sarbit, but he's been successfully running the Investors U.S. Growth Fund for several years. The fund has consistently been among the top performers in its category, producing an average annual rate of return of 19.5 percent for the five years to November 30, 1995. Sarbit is just one example of the many little-known fund managers with excellent credentials you can find by doing a bit of sleuthing.

Getting information about a fund's manager has become much easier. Manager profiles now appear regularly in the business pages of many major newspapers and in their monthly mutual fund supplements. In-depth analyses of individual funds and their management strategies have also become a business press fixture. There are several annual guides to mutual funds on the market, some of which contain profiles of leading fund managers. You can often dial in on the conference calls they hold regularly with sales representatives, or get a free audio cassette in which they explain their current outlook and strategy. So there's no shortage of information, if you're prepared to look for it.

There are two essential points to consider when assessing how a fund's manager is likely to perform. The first is past record. Check how the

trade talk

**ROBERT KREMBIL, TRIMARK**

Robert Krembil, head of the committees that manage the Trimark Fund, the Trimark Canadian Fund, and other related funds within the organization is probably the best-known committee manager in Canada.

Krembil is chairman of the board of Trimark, the company he co-founded in 1981. He's worked in the financial industry since 1964 and has managed investment portfolios for more than 25 years. Krembil takes a long-term view, looking for the companies with strong growth potential that can be held in a portfolio for many years. If you'd invested $10,000 in the Trimark Fund at its inception back in 1981, your money would be worth over $100,000 today. The other funds in the Trimark family are almost as impressive, which explains its status as one of the fastest-growing organizations in the country.

## trade talk

### IRWIN MICHAEL, ABC FUNDS

Irwin Michael is a young manager who's gaining public recognition. His two ABC rapidly growing funds have been performance leaders in their categories (Canadian equity and balanced) over the past five years. Michael, who blends a fundamentally conservative approach with the right degree of aggressiveness, is constantly on the lookout for good value; his uncanny ability to sniff it out has made his funds so successful.

If you want Michael's services, you'd better have at least $150,000. Michael is very protective of his clients, who are all serious, long-term investors. Even if you count yourself among this group, Michael will still turn you away if your investment represents too large a portion of your net worth. But once you get in, you have access to his attention, you receive his newsletter, and you have a stake in some compelling funds.

fund has done since the current manager took charge and how his or her performance compares with the fund's record prior to this time. If the fund's performance has improved or remained stable at an above-average level, it's a good sign (but, of course, no guarantee) for the future.

The second point to consider is stability. A manager who has been in place for several years and has produced good results is reassuring to potential investors. A new manager is an unknown quantity, unless he or she has established a track record with another fund.

Be extra cautious in the case of a fund that was run for several years by a manager who has recently departed. Caution is especially advisable if the manager was largely responsible for calling the shots (as opposed to working within a committee). In such cases, the fund's past record should be discounted when making a purchase decision.

A recent example of such a case was the departure of Barry Fierstein from the helm of the Bullock American Fund late in 1992. Bullock American had been one of my favourites for some time, but when Fierstein moved on it raised serious questions about the future. I stuck with the fund for a while (Fierstein hadn't moved anywhere that Canadian investors could follow him anyway). However, in mid-'93 it became very apparent to me that his successor, John Callaghan, was having trouble keeping up the standard of his predecessor. I recommended selling—a timely call, in retrospect, as the fund's annual return over the next two years was well below average for U.S. funds as a group and for small cap funds in particular.

## You shouldn't be in too much of a hurry to follow a departing manager.

As returns dropped, investors bailed out and the fund lost almost $100 million in assets. Some action was clearly needed. So in 1995 Spectrum United, the owners of Bullock American, came to the conclusion I had reached two years earlier and dismissed Callaghan as manager. Responsibility for the fund was handed over to MFS Asset Management, a Boston-based company, which happens to be a subsidiary of Sun Life Assurance—also the parent firm of Spectrum United. This was certainly no coincidence, but if it pays off with improved returns, investors won't complain.

Perhaps Fierstein's departure wasn't the sole cause for Bullock American going into a swoon, but it's an example of why it's important to reassess your position if a fund manager leaves.

Just don't react too quickly. Generally, the evidence suggests that you shouldn't be in too much of a hurry to follow a departing manager. Despite the experience of Bullock American, the fund that a departing manager has left behind sometimes performs better than the fund he takes over, at least for a while. For example, when highly regarded John Zechner left his position as manager of the Elliott & Page Equity Fund in mid-1993, there was much concern about its future prospects. Zechner later assumed responsibility for the new C.I. Canadian Growth Fund. He was replaced at

trade talk

## ALAN JACOBS,
## SCEPTRE EQUITY FUND

Young, dark, and intense, Alan Jacobs seems more like a movie star Wall Street baron than a Canadian money manager. But Jacobs is a rising star in the mutual fund industry, and the returns he's been generating with his Sceptre Equity Fund have attracted attention.

Jacobs is a value investor who goes for great companies that are selling at deep discounts. Sceptre focuses on small cap stocks which Jacobs sees as offering the greatest profit potential. But he's quick to point out that Sceptre is not just a small cap fund. There's a healthy mix of medium- and large-sized companies in the portfolio, making up about 40 percent of the holdings. Their presence adds stability by reducing the volatility that you usually see with small caps. The results speak for themselves. In the first two years after Jacobs took over, his fund gained an average of almost 21 percent a year.

E&P by Nereo Pittico, who took over at the end of '93.

What happened to the two funds during the period immediately following the changes? From the beginning of 1994 to September 30, 1995, Zechner's C.I. fund showed a total gain of 8.4 percent. If you'd moved $1,000 into it at the beginning of that period, you'd have owned units worth $1,084 21 months later. But if you'd left the money with E&P, your units would have been worth almost $1,113, for a total gain of 11.3 percent, a significantly higher gain than Zechner's new fund produced.

Similar situations occurred with the move of well-known manager Tony Massie from Sagit to Global Strategy and Gerald Coleman and Jerry Javasky from United to Mackenzie Financial, where they launched the Ivy funds. This doesn't mean a managerial change will always result in underperformance by the new fund or that the pattern will persist over time. But it suggests, at the very least, that it will take time for a manager to mould the new fund to his image and gather the momentum needed to generate above-average returns. The bottom line: if the manager moves, stick with the old fund for at least six months and then reassess the situation.

# All mutual funds contain a

measure of risk. The question is how much you're prepared to accept. . . . The more risk you take, the higher your potential returns should be and vice-versa. . . . Volatility is a good measure of risk, but it can be misleading at times. . . .

Let's deal with this issue right up front. If you're going to invest money in mutual funds, you have to accept a degree of risk. If you can't accept this fact, then keep your money in a savings account—although I have to tell you even that's not entirely risk-free.

But the mutual fund risk scale is very wide, ranging from minuscule risk to very high risk. You can pick any point on the scale that you like. If you want to keep risk to an absolute minimum, you can concentrate your investments in money market funds and mortgage funds. No money market fund sold in Canada has ever lost money for investors (although it could theoretically happen in certain extreme circumstances). Some mortgage funds may occasionally decline in value, but there are several that have never lost a dime in any calendar year since they were created—in some cases, this covers a span of more than two decades.

Another way to minimize risk is to invest in the segregated funds offered by insurance companies. All carry some degree of protection against loss, and in some cases the guarantee covers 100 percent of the amount you invest. See chapter 17 on segregated funds for more information.

But, as a general rule, the reality is that the less risk you take, the lower your potential returns. If you want above-average profits from your funds, then you'll have to crank up the risk level a few notches. It goes with the territory.

Clearly, the risk/return relationship must be a key consideration when you decide which mutual funds to buy. If preserving capital and avoiding loss is your prime concern, you'll select a conservative fund that shares these objectives. In this case, you'll give up some potential return for a higher measure of safety. On the other hand, if your objective is to maximize growth and you're willing to incur greater risk to achieve this, you'll search out more aggressively managed funds—and there are plenty around.

Certain types of mutual funds are better suited for conservative investors than others. The following table gives a general guideline of the risk/return relationship of various types of funds. Keep in mind, however, that there may be exceptions within any particular group. Review the prospectus of any fund you're interested in to be sure its goals match your own.

| Type of Fund | Risk Potential | Return Potential |
|---|---|---|
| Money Market | Low | Low |
| Mortgage | Low | Low/Medium |
| Bond | Low/Medium | Medium |
| Balanced | Medium | Medium |
| Dividend | Medium | Medium |
| Real Estate | Medium/High | Medium |
| International Equity (Broad-based) | Medium | Medium/High |
| U.S. Equity (Broad-based) | Medium/High | Medium/High |
| Canadian Equity (Broad-based) | Medium/High | Medium/High |
| International Equity (Regional) | High | High |
| Emerging Markets | High | High |
| Small Cap | High | High |
| Sector | High | High |
| Precious Metals | High | High |

You can determine a specific fund's risk potential through the use of a more precise measure known as *volatility* (also called *variability*), which has already been referred to briefly in chapter 5. Volatility is a mathematical calculation that measures the extent to which the actual monthly returns for a given fund swing up or down from its average return over a given period of time (usually three years).

Many people find this concept difficult to grasp, so look at it this way. Suppose a fund has an average rate of return of 1 percent a month over five years. This average could have been achieved through a series of sharp ups and downs—a gain of 10 percent one month, a loss of 8 percent the next, a jump of 5 percent the next, and so on. In this situation, the fund would be said to have a high volatility rating and the risk factor would be significant. However, if the actual returns throughout the whole period were exactly 1 percent each month, with no movement up or down, the fund would have a volatility rating of one (or 0.1 or zero, depending on the scale being used). This implies a very conservative management strategy and a correspondingly low risk rating.

know yourself

## HOW MUCH RISK IS TOO MUCH?

Want a quick insight into just how much of a risk-taker you are? Try this little self-test to find out.

A = Agree   D = Disagree   C = Unsure

| | |
|---|---|
| I enjoy visiting a casino and regard any losses as simply the cost of an evening's entertainment. | |
| I regularly buy lottery tickets. | _____ |
| When renewing a mortgage, I prefer to take a shorter term with a lower rate, rather than to lock in at a higher rate for five years. | _____ |
| When on the highway, I'll exceed the speed limit if no police are around. | _____ |
| I'd rather take a one in ten chance to win $5,000 than a one in three chance to win $500. | _____ |
| I enjoy playing games for money. | _____ |
| I delay planning holidays to the last minute in order to get discounts. | _____ |
| I usually arrive late for appointments. | _____ |
| I rarely worry about my investments. | _____ |
| I want to be rich and I'll do whatever it takes to achieve this, within reason. | _____ |

Score two points for every "Agree," one point for each "Unsure," and no points for all "Disagree" responses. Here's how to interpret the results.

15-20 points–You like to live on the edge. You have a high tolerance for risk and should plan your mutual fund investments accordingly.

8-14 points–You'll accept a degree of risk, but it may make you somewhat uncomfortable and you don't want to overdo it. A balanced fund portfolio looks appropriate.

0-7 points–You're very conservative by nature. Too much risk will give you bad dreams. Stick with funds at the lowest end of the risk scale.

the fine print

**STANDARD DEVIATION**

The monthly performance tables published by *The Financial Post* include a column showing the standard deviation of a fund relative to all the others in the group for the past three years. The higher this number, the greater a fund's volatility. For example, to the end of November 1995, the *Post* reported that the Cambridge Special Equity Fund scored 9.1 on their standard deviation scale, making it the most volatile Canadian equity fund reported. (The average was 3.3.) Least volatile was the Admax Canadian Select Growth Fund, with a score of 1.4. (Just to show you that volatility and return don't necessarily go hand-in-hand, the steady Admax Fund produced an average annual compound rate of return of only 5.5 percent during that three-year period. The roller coaster Cambridge Fund rewarded its stout-hearted investors with a 36.6 percent annual return.)

The concept of volatility is useful, but it must be combined with a little common sense. For example, most money market funds have volatility ratings of 0.1 in *The Financial Post*. This is because of the low-risk nature of their investments: Treasury bills, term deposits, and high-quality short-term corporate notes. An investment portfolio of this type is as close to risk-free as you'll find and churns out consistent returns month after month. Since volatility scores put a premium on such virtues, money market funds rank highly.

If volatility were the only criterion, everyone would have all their cash in money market funds. However, there are other things to consider. The low volatility score achieved by money market funds correctly highlights their safety but disguises the fact that their growth potential is nil and their income potential declines as interest rates fall. They will always perform well relative to risk, because the risk is almost non-existent. But they cannot achieve the growth potential of an equity fund or even a bond fund. So don't get so carried away with studying volatility ratings that you lose sight of the underlying characteristics of the fund itself.

There are three other criteria to use to determine the risk/return potential of a given fund. One is to carefully study the section of the prospectus on management objectives. Phrases such as "will seek to maximize growth," "aggressive management approach," or "emphasis will be on above-average capital gains" indicate that you're dealing with a higher risk fund.

The second is to review the annual performance record of the fund, going back 10 to 15 years. *The Globe and Mail* and *The Financial Post* publish this information periodically. You can also find it in Southam's *Mutual Fund SourceBook.* The book is expensive, but you may be able to borrow a copy at a library or from your mutual fund salesperson. The *SourceBook* contains the annual performance records of most Canadian mutual funds. I look especially for losing years; funds that rarely suffer a loss over any 12-month period appeal strongly to me regardless of their volatility rating.

trade talk

**THE OTHER END**

It's not something they're anxious to publicize, but the worst-performing broadly based Canadian equity funds over the five-year period to November 30, 1995, were the Hodgson Roberton Laing Canadian Fund with a 4.1 percent average annual compound rate of return; the CIBC Canadian Equity Fund, 4.5 percent; the Trans-Canada Equity Fund, 5.5 percent; the Top Fifty Equity Fund, 6 percent; and the MetLife MVP Equity Fund, 6.1 percent. The only good news is that at least they all made money.

An analysis of how well the funds you're considering performed over time will provide some valuable insights into how the managers cope with adversity.

Finally, in the case of equity funds, I look for those that have stood up especially well in difficult conditions. For ex-

trade talk

**TOUGHING IT OUT**

Trimark Canadian is one example of a fund that holds up well during tough years. It posted a gain of 6.6 percent in 1987, the year of the big stock market crash. In 1992 and 1994, both years when the TSE 300 lost ground, the fund came out ahead with advances of 6.6 percent and 2.5 percent, respectively. The only losing year over the decade was 1990, when the unit value dropped 12.1 percent. But that was better than the TSE 300, which lost 14.8 percent that year.

ample, 1994 was a tough year for both bond and stock markets. See which funds held up best during those hard times. Then review some earlier difficult years. Both 1990 and 1992 were down years for the TSE 300; see which Canadian stock funds did best then.

An analysis of how well the funds you're considering performed over time will provide some valuable insights into how the managers cope with adversity. Using figures from *The Globe and Mail*, I've prepared a list of the top five performers among broadly based Canadian equity funds during the period from December 1, 1990, to November 30, 1995, based on the average compound annual rate of return you would have received had you invested at the beginning of the period. The results may surprise you.

| Fund | Annual Return* (1990–1995) |
|---|---|
| Marathon Equity | 31.5% |
| Multiple Opportunities | 28.6% |
| ABC Fundamental Value | 28.1% |
| Altamira Equity | 25.0% |
| AIC Advantage | 24.1% |

\* Average annual compound rate of return

Although 1993 and 1995 were good to Canadian stock investors, the rest of the five-year period was tough. The fact that each of these funds generated average profits well in excess of 20 percent a year is a testament to good management.

It's important to note that most of these top performers are more volatile than the average Canadian equity fund. The AIC and ABC funds both score "High" on *The Globe and Mail* scale. The other three rank as "Above Average" in their volatility. This confirms that if you want top returns, you may have to put up with increased volatility— in other words, higher risk.

One technique some fund companies use to allay customers' concerns about risk is to obtain a rating from one of the Canadian bond rating services. The Bank of Commerce has done this with its money market, fixed income, and balanced funds (most received the top rating). Investors Group and the Bank of Montreal have also had some of their funds rated (again, all received the top mark or close to it).

All these ratings mean, however, is that the fund invests in high-quality securities—in other words, the portfolio itself is relatively low risk. The rating says nothing about the ability of the fund managers to produce superior returns, nor does it suggest the fund won't lose money in a bad investment climate. It's simply a comment on the strength of the securities being held, nothing more.

# Choosing a strategy and

sticking to it is a prerequisite for making money in funds. . . . Switching strategies is becoming popular in Canada, but watch out for the tax trap. . . . Leveraging offers the potential to pyramid your gains—but if you guess wrong, the losses will mount up so fast you won't believe it. . . .

It would be great if all there was to mutual fund investing was deciding you wanted to do it and then going out and picking a few funds. Unfortunately, as with everything else in life, it's more complicated than this. In fact, there are five key components to making money in mutual funds:

1. Deciding to actually invest in funds and committing money.
2. Determining which types of funds are best for you.
3. Understanding the principles of picking winning funds.
4. Deciding on a comfortable strategy. (This is the stage we're at in this chapter.)
5. Building a portfolio.

The strategy issue is critical. Investing in mutual funds involves more than just buying a few funds and settling back in the hope that your returns will be good. The right strategy provides a framework and a direction for your entire mutual fund program. A number of strategies are available to you. Which one you select at the outset will depend on your personality and objectives. But decide on a course before you start; don't flounder around in uncertainty. You can always move in another direction later or even mix strategies once you feel comfortable with what you're doing. At the beginning, though, decide on one strategy and stick to it for at least a year. Your options include:

## BUY AND HOLD

This is the easiest strategy of all, so it's highly suitable for beginners. It simply involves buying and holding units in carefully selected mutual funds, adding to your portfolio when you wish. This approach is consistent with the attitude you should be taking towards mutual funds: they represent a long-term investment in your future. With the exception of money market funds and resource funds, I rarely buy into a fund I am not prepared to hold for at least five years.

## DOLLAR-COST AVERAGING

A more disciplined variation of the buy-and-hold approach is dollar-cost averaging. This involves investing a given amount of money in the funds of your choice at periodic intervals—monthly, quarterly, semi-annually, or annually.

The benefits of this strategy are two-fold. First, it creates a system of forced savings, a discipline many investors need. Second, it reduces risk. If you stick to your plan, you'll avoid the classic investment trap of buying high and selling low. The

**inside info**

## USE SOME COMMON SENSE

As with any other investment strategy, you should temper a buy-and-hold approach with common sense. As long as a fund is generating an above-average return for its type, you should continue to hold it. However, if performance slips below average for 18 months or more, you should review the situation. Inquire about the fund management. Find out if key personnel have changed or if there has been a shift in investment philosophy. Ask for explanations of why the fund has underperformed. If you're not satisfied with the answers, the time has come to put your money elsewhere.

peaks and valleys will be automatically evened out. Of course, this also means your return won't be as high, but that's the price you pay for lower risk.

The psychology of this strategy is important. When the unit price of an equity fund is low, it probably means the stock market has fallen. This often scares off small investors who, in fact, should be taking advantage of the opportunity to add to their holdings at bargain prices. When unit prices are high, it probably means the market is going through a bullish phase—a time when many investors get carried away with enthusiasm and commit too much cash. Dollar-cost averaging acts as a discipline against these natural tendencies, which is why many investors swear by it.

To understand how dollar-cost averaging works, take a look at the following simplified example. I've assumed an investor who has decided to put $500 every quarter into a hypothetical no-load equity fund.

| Date of Purchase | Amount Invested | Unit Price | Number Bought | Total Owned | Market Value |
|---|---|---|---|---|---|
| Jan. 1, '96 | $500 | $10 | 50.00 | 50.00 | $500.00 |
| Apr. 1, '96 | 500 | 9 | 55.56 | 105.56 | 950.04 |
| Jul. 1, '96 | 500 | 11 | 45.45 | 151.01 | 1,661.11 |
| Oct. 1, '96 | 500 | 12 | 41.67 | 192.68 | 2,312.16 |

As you can see, during 1996 the price he will pay for units in the fund ranges from a low of $9 to a high of $12. When the price is low, he acquires more units for his $500; when it is high, he receives fewer. The average cost of the 192.68 units he purchases during 1996 works out to $10.38 each; the per unit value at year-end is $12. So he's made an average profit of $1.62 per unit over the year.

Obviously, this investor would be better off buying all his units on April 1, when the price is lowest. But there is no way to predict this in advance. Dollar-cost averaging enables you to take advantage of price dips when they occur while preventing you from over-investing when prices are high.

## the fine print

**BULLS AND BEARS**

A bull market is a period when most securities of a certain type are rising in price. The term is usually associated with the stock market, but in fact a bull market can occur in any investment area. There can be a bull market in bonds, in real estate, in gold, in lumber futures, and so on. Bull markets in different investment areas may occur simultaneously or at completely different times. There can also be bull markets at different times in overseas markets; thus Japan's Nikkei Index might be in a bull phase while the Paris Bourse is falling. The opposite of a bull market is a bear market—a time when declining prices create opportunities for bargain hunters.

SWITCHING

For some investors, buy-and-hold and dollar-cost averaging strategies are too tame. They want more action and faster growth, and they're willing to take the risks associated with this. They also believe they can time market movements, at least to some extent. So they use a switching strategy and move their money among different types of mutual funds depending on conditions.

This approach to fund investing is more common in the United States, where there are many large mutual fund companies that offer a wide variety of funds and charge very low fees (or none at all) to switch your money among them. So widespread has switching become south of the border that many investment newsletters focus exclusively on the subject.

In Canada, your options have been somewhat limited, but more fund companies are now recognizing the growing importance of switching to many investors. As a result, they've aggressively added to the number of funds they offer, thus giving switchers more choice. Companies are also removing some of the impediments to easy switching.

For example, Mackenzie Financial Corporation operates three distinct groups of mutual funds: the Industrial

Group, the Ivy Group, and the Universal Group. Until recently, however, a Chinese wall stood between them; if you held units in one group, you could not switch to another. You had to sell your holdings, perhaps paying a stiff back-end load in the process, and then make a new purchase in the group you wanted to get into—paying a new commission, of course. This clearly discouraged switching, and probably cost Mackenzie business as a result. But now the walls are down, and Mackenzie has become a switcher's paradise with more than 30 funds and three distinct managerial styles from which to choose. You can move among all three Mackenzie families without restriction other than the nominal 2 percent switching fee your sales rep is allowed to charge (and which you may be able to negotiate down to zero).

Of course, the no-load funds, such as those offered by financial institutions and fund companies like Altamira, Phillips, Hager & North, and Scudder, allow free switching among all their funds.

The dedicated switcher will search out companies that combine an attractive switching policy with high-performance funds. This is why it's especially important for

danger zone

**A TAX TRAP**

A major impediment to switching in this country is the government's view that any movement of assets from one mutual fund to another constitutes a sale and a purchase for tax purposes. This means that if your units have increased in value since you bought them, a switch will trigger a taxable capital gain unless it takes place inside a tax-sheltered plan such as an RRSP. To combat this, a few companies, including AGF, C.I., and G.T. Global, have set up umbrella funds composed of different "sectors," each with its own area of investment specialization. Switching assets from one sector to another does not trigger a capital gain, because the transaction takes place within the single umbrella fund. So, for example, you could move from C.I. Sector Pacific to C.I. Sector Emerging Markets without incurring a tax liability. But if you tried to do the same thing in the company's regular funds, you'd be looking at a taxable gain.

switchers to carefully review the entire family and not base their investment decision on the performance of a single fund.

A basic switching strategy involves being heavily invested in equity funds at times when the stock market is in a bullish phase and switching into money market and/or fixed income funds at other times. The trick, obviously, is to get out of the equity funds before the stock market tumbles. If you're not confident of your ability to do this, a switching strategy probably isn't right for you.

More sophisticated switching strategies involve moving money around in different international funds, increasing holdings in countries that look like their markets are in a bull phase and moving out of high risk areas. This is very tough to do on a consistent basis, however. In fact, if you develop a knack for it, you should probably apply for a job as a fund manager yourself.

## ASSET MIX

An alternative to switching for those who want to increase the growth potential of their funds is an asset mix approach. This involves structuring your fund portfolio in such a way as to give certain types of investments greater weight than others, in line with current economic conditions.

The true asset mix investor will always hold some funds from each of the three key asset groups in his or her portfolio. The percentage of each will be shifted periodically, depending on a number of factors including age, risk tolerance, and general economic conditions. For example, a younger person who wishes to emphasize growth might use the following asset mix during good economic times:

| | |
|---|---|
| Cash-type funds | 5% – 15% |
| Fixed income funds | 15% – 25% |
| Growth funds | 60% – 80% |

When the economy is heading for rougher times and the stock market looks vulnerable, this investor might vary the asset mix as follows:

| | |
|---|---|
| Cash-type funds | 25% – 40% |
| Fixed income funds | 25% – 50% |
| Growth funds | 30% – 50% |

The latter variation produces a more balanced mix and reduces the fund's exposure to the stock market while allowing the build-up of cash reserves to take advantage of future buying opportunities. The fixed income section is also strengthened because deteriorating economic times frequently signal a drop in interest rates. This will have a positive effect on the unit values of bond funds and, to a lesser extent, mortgage funds.

Varying your asset mix can be achieved by using switching techniques, as long as this can be done at minimal cost. It can also be done by directing new investment money to the asset categories you wish to strengthen.

the fine print

**ASSET TYPES**

There are three types of investments in a basic asset mix:

Cash or equivalent—These are highly liquid, low-risk investments. T-bill and money market funds are used here.

Fixed income—These are investments in securities that pay a fixed rate of return on your money. Bond and mortgage funds would qualify in this group, as would some (but not all) dividend income funds.

Growth—These are investments that depend mainly on capital gains for profit, such as equity and precious metals funds.

## LEVERAGING

Leveraging involves increasing your profit potential by using someone else's money. Leveraging allows you to increase your bottom-line return significantly. However, it's not as easy as it may seem at first glance.

Leveraging works two ways. It will increase your returns when investments perform well. But it can leave you twisting in the wind if things turn sour. Let's look at the two sides of the leveraging coin.

Suppose you want to build a mutual fund portfolio but you have only $10,000 to invest. If you decide to invest this money, and nothing more, here's how you'd make out with a fund that grows at a rate of 10 percent annually, compounded. (For simplicity, I've left taxes out of the calculation.)

| INITIAL INVESTMENT | VALUE AFTER 1 YEAR | VALUE AFTER 3 YEARS | VALUE AFTER 5 YEARS |
|---|---|---|---|
| $10,000 | $11,000 | $13,310 | $16,105 |

Looks pretty good—after five years your asset base has increased more than 60 percent. If you sold your fund portfolio at this time, you'd walk away with a profit of $6,105.

Now, suppose you borrowed an additional $10,000 from the bank at 8 percent annual interest to add to your investment capital. Since the loan is for investment purposes, the interest is tax-deductible. If you're in a 50 percent tax bracket, the true after-tax interest rate you pay is actually only 4 percent. By taking this loan, you increase your initial investment to $20,000. Here's how your results would look in this situation:

| INITIAL INVESTMENT | VALUE AFTER 1 YEAR | VALUE AFTER 3 YEARS | VALUE AFTER 5 YEARS |
|---|---|---|---|
| $20,000 | $22,000 | $26,620 | $32,210 |

Again, let's assume you liquidate your portfolio after five years. Here's what happens:

| | |
|---|---|
| Proceeds from the sale | $32,210 |
| After-tax interest charges | (2,000) |
| Repayment of loan principal | (10,000) |
| Net proceeds | $20,210 |
| Profit on $10,000 investment | $10,210 |

Leveraging has paid off very handsomely in this situation. By using other people's money, you've increased your overall return by more than $4,000 and the percentage return on your own money has jumped from about 60 percent to more than 100 percent. If it's so easy then, why doesn't everyone do it?

Because there's a dark side to the moon, that's why. Yes, everything is rosy if your funds go up. But what happens if they drop in value? Suppose, for example, your fund loses 5 percent a year instead of showing a profit. Here's what happens if you put up your own money only:

| INITIAL INVESTMENT | VALUE AFTER 1 YEAR | VALUE AFTER 3 YEARS | VALUE AFTER 5 YEARS |
|---|---|---|---|
| $10,000 | $9,500 | $8,574 | $7,738 |

Your loss at the end of five years is $2,262.

Now, here's what happens if you borrow an additional $10,000 and add it to your own stake:

| INITIAL INVESTMENT | VALUE AFTER 1 YEAR | VALUE AFTER 3 YEARS | VALUE AFTER 5 YEARS |
|---|---|---|---|
| $20,000 | $19,000 | $17,148 | $15,476 |

In this case, when you liquidate your holdings after five years your results will be as follows:

| | |
|---|---|
| Gross proceeds of sale | $15,476 |
| After-tax interest charges | (2,000) |
| Repayment of loan principal | (10,000) |
| Net proceeds | $ 3,476 |
| Loss on original $10,000 | $ 6,524 |

Your loss is almost three times as great as it would have been had you not leveraged your investment. So, as you can clearly see, a leveraging strategy can be risky business. High-rollers looking for big returns sometimes finance part of their mutual fund investments with borrowed money. But this is not a recommended strategy for beginning fund investors. If your investments don't perform well, you could face heavy losses and you'd probably end up hating mutual funds for the rest of your life. Leveraging should only be used by experienced people who clearly understand the potential dangers involved and accept them.

# Mutual funds can add

profit potential to your RRSP—or blow your retirement plan out of the water. . . . One big advantage of funds is flexibility. You can move your money any time, although it may cost you something. . . . You can hold up to 20 percent of your RRSP money in foreign funds. Some companies will keep a computer watch on your portfolio to make sure you don't stray over the line. . . .

If you're concerned about paying less tax, or having enough money to live on when you retire, or both, you probably have an RRSP. And, if you're like millions of other Canadians, you probably know very little about it (take the self-test on page 98 to see how much you know).

This isn't a book about RRSPs as such, so I'm not going to devote much space to the subject. (If you want detailed insights about how to run an effective retirement plan, pick up a copy of *Retiring Wealthy* and/or *Gordon Pape's Buyer's Guide to RRSPs*.) But I think it's important to spend a few pages discussing the use of mutual funds in an RRSP, because it's a mixture that has the potential either to make your retirement years much more comfortable or to blow your dreams out of the water and force you to keep working until age 80.

For starters, not every RRSP can be used to hold mutual funds. Only two types of plans enable you do to this.

## HOW MUCH DO YOU KNOW ABOUT YOUR RRSP?

Take the following self-test. Then rate your score at the bottom.

|  | Yes | No |
|---|---|---|
| I know the total value of all my RRSPs within $500. | ____ | ____ |
| I know what return my RRSPs earned last year. | ____ | ____ |
| I know what assets I have in all my RRSPs. | ____ | ____ |
| I know without looking it up how many RRSPs I have and where they are located. | ____ | ____ |
| I know where to invest this year's RRSP contribution to improve my returns. | ____ | ____ |
| I know the percentage of foreign content in my RRSPs. | ____ | ____ |
| I know how much I can contribute to my RRSP this year. | ____ | ____ |

Score one point for every "yes" answer, zero for each "no." Here's how to interpret the results:

6-7 points—You're right on top of your retirement plan and have a clear idea of what you're doing.

4-5 points—You're making an effort, but more attention is needed.

2-3 points—A little knowledge is better than none—but it's not good enough.

0-1 points—You haven't a clue.

## MUTUAL FUND PLANS

These are RRSPs set up by mutual fund companies and financial institutions for the specific purpose of enabling you to buy their funds for your retirement plan. There is usually an annual trustee fee ($25–$50 plus GST) attached to these plans but there are no other special fees. These plans are usually (but not always) restricted to the funds offered by the sponsoring company.

## SELF-DIRECTED PLANS

A self-directed plan enables you to hold any RRSP-eligible security, including mutual funds. In theory, therefore, you should be able to put any mutual fund you want into a self-directed plan. In reality, however, it doesn't work out this way. If you set up such a plan with a broker or financial planner, he'll be reluctant to acquire no-load funds for you because he receives no sales commission. Discount brokers, like Green Line, will let you purchase such funds, but you'll have to pay a sales commission or redemption charge, which of course defeats the main attraction of no-load funds. If you open the plan at a bank, you may encounter some resistance if you try to acquire units in another bank's funds. So while a self-directed plan gives you more flexibility, you'll still find some restrictions. Fees typically run around $125 a year.

There are several advantages to including mutual funds in an RRSP portfolio. For one, this is the most effective way to diversify your retirement plan. Adding funds to your mix allows you to introduce some growth potential into your plan, which GICs don't offer. Funds also enable you to, in effect, move some of your RRSP assets outside Canada through the use of international funds. This gives you a measure of protection against the ups and downs of the Canadian dollar and allows you to profit from faster economic growth in other parts of the world.

Mutual funds also substantially increase the profit potential of your RRSP. If you'd invested all your money in GICs over the five years ending September 30, 1995, your average annual return would have been 10.6 percent. That's not bad. But the average bond mutual fund did slightly better during that period (10.8 percent). And the top performing bond funds like Altamira Income and Phillips, Hager & North Bond (both of which I've consistently recommended in my annual *Buyer's Guide to Mutual Funds*) did much better at 14 percent and 12.8 percent, respectively.

The third major benefit of mutual funds in an RRSP is flexibility. If you don't like the way things are going, you can simply switch your assets to another fund. You can't do this with a GIC, which locks you in until maturity.

the fine print

**THE SHELL GAME**

Registered Retirement Savings Plans (RRSPs) are not an investment in themselves, contrary to what many people believe. ("My RRSP is maturing next month," really means, "The GIC in the RRSP is maturing.") Think of an RRSP as a tax-sheltered empty shell into which you can place almost any type of security you wish. Mutual funds licensed for sale in Canada are just one of the many securities that qualify.

It's true that you're supposed to take a long-term view when making RRSP investment decisions. But tomorrow's vision of the future may be quite different from today's. Having the flexibility to meet changing conditions is a big advantage in any investment situation.

But there are disadvantages to holding mutual funds in your retirement plan. It's important to understand them and

## inside info

### A TAX BREAK!

Although you can't pay sales commissions outside your RRSP, you can pay the annual administration fee this way. If you do, it's tax deductible, as a "carrying charge." But watch out. Some companies automatically deduct the administration fee from your plan without advising you. In this case, you can't claim any tax relief. If you notice such a deduction on your RRSP statement, send the company a cheque to cover the amount and ask them to recredit your plan with the money they withdrew.

to weigh all the pros and cons before plunging ahead. One consideration is the expense. Mutual funds will cost your RRSP some money. It may be no more than an annual trustee charge plus the management fees that are deducted from the assets of the funds you hold. Or your costs may include some hefty sales commissions, depending on the type of funds you purchase. Unfortunately, these commissions have to be paid from within the RRSP. I've tried on several occasions to persuade a broker to let me pay sales commissions outside my retirement plan, without any luck. Bureaucracy won't allow it to happen.

The other potential big disadvantage is losses. I said previously that adding mutual funds to your RRSP has the potential to blow your retirement plan out of the water. But only—I stress *only*—if you are careless or unwise in your investments.

Here's an example of how you can go wrong. In 1993–94, a new type of mutual fund burst on to the Canadian scene—the Latin American fund. Suddenly people were going ga-ga over the exciting growth prospects of Mexico and points south of there. The land of siestas and swaying palms had been magically transformed into the new investment mecca.

I was concerned about the whole phenomenon. It seemed to be a lot of hype. In my *1995 Buyer's Guide to Mutual Funds* (which came out in the fall of 1994), I wrote, "The reality is that Latin American markets are thin and volatile. The economies will gyrate like lambada dancers at an all-night cantina with every political downturn or the poor performance of a few key stocks. The return potential is above average, but these markets are not for the faint of heart." RRSP mutual funds should be restricted to those that are conservatively managed, well diversified, and have low volatility. Your retirement capital should not be used for speculation.

Now, tell me. Does this sound to you like the type of mutual fund you should be putting into a retirement plan? If it does, then stay well away from mutual funds in your RRSP. You're a clear "blow-your-self-out-of-the-water" candidate.

Unfortunately, I've encountered many people who did indeed add Latin funds to their RRSPs as foreign content. After the crash, they asked me what to do, which is sort of like deciding to take out fire insurance after the house has burned to the ground.

trade talk

**LATIN BLOWOUT**

The unexpected collapse of the Mexican peso in late 1994 and the subsequent recession that gripped that country (the worst since World War II) sent shock waves through all of Latin America and scorched the new mutual funds that had been created to channel Canadian money to that part of the world. Over the one-year period to October 31, 1995, the 20/20 Latin America Fund lost 25.8 percent of its value, the C.I. Latin American Fund dropped 34.6 percent, the Hercules Latin America Fund fell 40.4 percent, and Fidelity's Latin American Growth Fund was down 42.4 percent.

## RRSP mutual funds should be restricted to those that are conservatively managed, well diversified, and have low volatility. Your retirement capital should not be used for speculation.

## CHECK YOUR STATEMENT

Many companies show only the current market value of your RRSP on the statements you receive, not the book value. This makes it virtually impossible to keep track of your foreign content percentage. If your plan isn't automatically monitored and you're not getting this information, you may have to take your business elsewhere.

RRSP mutual funds should be restricted to those that are conservatively managed, well diversified, and have low volatility. Your retirement capital should not be used for speculation. Sure, you want to improve returns relative to those offered by CSBs and GICs. But your number one priority is to preserve your capital. Select your funds on this basis or look for other options.

One other point about mutual funds in an RRSP. This is the simplest way to add foreign content to your plan, but make sure you understand the rules. You're allowed to hold up to 20 percent of the book value of your RRSP in international securities. If you go beyond this, Revenue Canada hits you with penalty interest of 1 percent a month on the excess. Book value is simply the original price you paid for any securities in your plan. The current value—what they could be sold for today—is known as the market value. It's possible for your RRSP foreign content to exceed 20 percent of market value (for example, if your foreign funds have increased sharply in price). But this is not a problem, as long as your book value stays on side.

You shouldn't have to worry about keeping your foreign content within the legal limit. Many RRSP administrators now automatically monitor your foreign holdings and advise you promptly if you stray over the boundary. Some will even automatically rebalance your plan if you get offside by selling enough foreign fund units to bring you back within the limit. But not every organization has computer programs that are this sophisticated yet. So if you're planning to add foreign funds to your RRSP, be sure to ask about the monitoring practices of the plan administrator. If they're not equipped to keep your plan on track, be prepared to do it yourself.

# There's no such thing as

an "ideal" fund portfolio—it all comes down to what you want to achieve. . . . You may not be able to add the specific fund you want to your portfolio—restrictions may get in the way. . . . You can take a lazy approach and use an asset allocation service, but you may not get the portfolio you need. . . .

By this point, you should be familiar with the basic principles of selecting winning mutual funds. You should also have a sense of which types of funds are best for your needs and the strategy that you'll feel most comfortable with. Now it's a case of using your knowledge to construct a full mutual fund portfolio that will provide the diversity and the flexibility you need. In a perfect world, this would mean putting together a portfolio of the top mutual funds in the country that meet your selection criteria, wherever they are to be found. In reality, however, this simply isn't possible. Several obstacles lie in the way of the dream portfolio, including:

### PLAN RESTRICTIONS

The structure of your mutual fund plan probably won't give you the total flexibility you need to create an ideal portfolio. For example, if you're dealing inside a registered plan (RRSP, RRIF, etc.) your foreign content will be limited by the 20 percent rule. Or, as explained in the previous chapter, if you're building your fund portfolio using the services of a broker or financial planner, you may not be able to add no-load funds to the mix.

## SALES RESTRICTIONS

Some companies make their funds available only to clients who set up an account with them. This includes life insurance firms and financial planning organizations like Investors Group.

 danger zone

**CLOSED FOR BUSINESS**

Managers will occasionally close a fund to investors, which can be very frustrating if you've put it on your wish list. These closures can be temporary or permanent. One example: in late 1995, the Cundill Security Fund was temporarily closed because of a high cash position, in excess of 40 percent. Since rates at the time were low, the interest being earned by the cash deposits was minimal, thus reducing the returns for existing investors. As a result, the managers announced that no new money would be accepted until suitable investments were found for most of the spare cash.

## TERRITORIAL RESTRICTIONS

Some companies are not registered to sell their funds across Canada. As a result, they're not available in certain provinces. The speculative Multiple Opportunities Fund, for example, can only be purchased by residents of British Columbia.

## COMPANY RESTRICTIONS

A number of firms only make certain funds available to people who meet some other requirement. For example, the Industrial Cash Management Fund has been one of my top selections in the money market fund category for several years. But it's only open to investors who buy Mackenzie Financial funds on a front-end load basis.

## PROFESSIONAL RESTRICTIONS

Certain funds are only available to people in a specific profession. There are exclusive funds for pilots, dentists, teachers, engineers, doctors, etc. If you're not in the right group, you obviously can't include any of these in your mix.

## PRACTICAL RESTRICTIONS

Many people only want to deal with one or two mutual fund organizations. Keeping track of more than that gets too complicated. This means their portfolio will be restricted to funds offered by these particular companies.

Because of these restrictions you will have to make compromises in building your mutual fund portfolio. But don't let this deter you. Even if you can't put together what you think is an ideal plan, you can come fairly close.

One of the keys to building a good portfolio is to recognize the strengths and weaknesses of the particular fund universe that's available to you. To show you what I mean, let's look at one of the big bank groups—CIBC Securities. A lot of people have their money here: As of November 1995, CIBC was the fifth-largest mutual fund group in Canada, with assets under management of $6.2 billion. One big attraction of CIBC (as with all the bank groups) is convenience. It's the one-stop shopping concept: you can make a deposit and then walk down to the next counter for mutual fund information.

Many people obviously do exactly that, and it may be that CIBC funds are the only ones they own. If so, they need to carefully consider how they construct their portfolio, because, over the years, CIBC has built a very poor record with its equity funds. For example, their flagship stock fund, the CIBC Canadian Equity Fund, produced an average annual return of only 4.5 percent for the five

trade talk

**PLAYING CATCH-UP**

With competition for mutual fund dollars heating up, CIBC was well aware of its deficiencies compared to the other big banks. Late in 1995 the company decided to deal with the problem by hiring Paul Starita, the architect of the highly successful Royal Trust fund group, to run the show. Given his track record, CIBC funds should become a much more exciting place to have your money in the late '90s.

years ending November 30, 1995. This was the second-worst return in its category during this period.

## CIBC's equity funds have been indifferent performers over the years. But the bank's fixed income funds have done quite well for investors.

On the other hand, some of the bank's fixed income funds have been pretty good performers. The CIBC Mortgage Investment Fund, to name one, is consistently among the leaders in its category and has a long record of solid, dependable returns.

The message here should be obvious. If you want to build a portfolio with above-average growth potential, you should not be using CIBC funds to do it. Although the bank is taking steps to improve their equity funds, they still have a lot to prove. But if your goal is a conservative, low-risk income portfolio, then CIBC can do the job very nicely. Here's an example of what such a portfolio might look like:

| Fund | % of Portfolio |
|---|---|
| T-bill | 10% |
| U.S. Money Market | 10% |
| Mortgage | 20% |
| Canadian Income | 15% |
| Global Bond Fund | 10% |
| Balanced Income and Growth | 15% |
| U.S. Equity | 10% |
| Canadian Equity | 10% |

Here we have a portfolio that has a high degree of safety, with 65 percent of the assets in money market and fixed income funds—the areas where CIBC historically performs best. The rest is invested in funds with growth potential—not a lot, but this is a conservative portfolio for a low-risk investor.

Now let's look at another no-load fund group, Altamira. Here we're faced with quite a different situation. While Altamira does have some good fixed income funds, they tend to be more aggressively managed for higher returns. This means they also carry a greater degree of risk. As well, Altamira doesn't offer some of the key funds conservative investors might want, such as a mortgage fund. The company's great strength is its equity funds, some of which have been top performers for most of this decade.

**TOP PERFORMER**

The Altamira Equity Fund was one of the top performers in Canada over the five-year period to November 30, 1995. Its average annual compound rate of return during that time was 25 percent. This means if you'd made an investment on December 1, 1990, you'd have tripled your money in just five years!

Conclusion: this is a good company to work with if you want to build a fund portfolio with excellent growth potential. It's not a very good choice for conservative investors, however. They'll probably feel more comfortable with CIBC.

Here's an example of an aggressive Altamira portfolio.

| FUND | % OF PORTFOLIO |
| --- | --- |
| Cash Account | 5% |
| Global Money | 10% |
| Income | 10% |
| Growth and Income | 10% |
| Equity | 20% |
| Special Growth | 5% |
| Resource | 5% |
| Precious and Strategic Metals | 5% |
| Asia Pacific | 10% |
| Select American | 10% |
| Europe | 10% |

This is a broadly diversified portfolio with a variety of funds both domestic and international in their focus.

There's quite a bit of risk here—the Resource, Precious and Strategic Metals, Special Growth, and Asia-Pacific funds all have the potential for both above-average gains and above-average losses. But for an investor who understands and accepts this, an Altamira portfolio can be exciting.

Now let's look at a portfolio with some built-in restrictions, such as you'd find in a registered retirement savings plan. In this case, you want to build a low-risk portfolio (you shouldn't be taking many chances with your retirement money) and you're limited in the amount of foreign content you can hold. Let's say that you're using a self-directed RRSP, which means your selection is much greater. This type of fund portfolio might end up looking like the following one.

| FUND | % OF PORTFOLIO |
|------|----------------|
| Sceptre Money Market | 10% |
| First Canadian Mortgage | 20% |
| Altamira Income | 20% |
| Dynamic Global Bond | 10% |
| Trimark RSP Equity | 20% |
| Trimark Fund | 10% |
| Templeton Growth | 10% |

Here we've put together a portfolio that includes top-performing funds from several companies. We've maximized the foreign content by placing 10 percent of the portfolio into each of Trimark Fund and Templeton Growth Fund (Dynamic Global Bond Fund qualifies as Canadian content despite the name). The result is an RRSP portfolio that offers a good asset mix, conservatively managed funds and above-average growth potential. All the funds in the sample RRSP portfolio have consistently received high ratings in my annual *Buyer's Guide to RRSPs*. If you'd built an RRSP portfolio such as this, your one-year return to November 30, 1995, would have been 14.7 percent.

Many other portfolio combinations are possible, depending on your needs. You might want to build a portfolio to generate the maximum possible tax-sheltered income, or one that's suited for an RRIF, or one that maximizes growth potential. There's a universe of choices.

There is a lazy person's approach to all this. You could simply use a mutual fund asset allocation service or invest only in balanced funds. But you might end up with a one-size-fits-all type of portfolio that wouldn't meet your specific needs.

It takes some time and thought to construct a solid personal portfolio. But it's well worth the effort.

trade talk

**UPS AND DOWNS**

The Altamira Resource Fund is a classic example of a boom or bust type of investment. It struggled through 1994 and 1995—the two-year return to November 30, 1995, showed an average annual loss of 3.1 percent. But if you'd put money into the fund on December 1, 1990, you'd be showing an average annual gain of more than 25 percent over the five-year period—thanks to huge back-to-back returns of 64 and 65 percent in 1992-93.

# Avoid making errors in

fund investing that can end up being very expensive.
Here are 10 to avoid. . . . The fund world is complex and
constantly changing. Get some professional advice or do
a lot of homework. . . . If you're conservative by nature,
stick to funds that are low risk. Don't be sucked in by
hype. . . .

So far, this book has focused mainly on the positive—the basic principles of successful mutual fund investing. In this chapter we look at
some of the pitfalls and how to avoid them. Here's a summary of the 10
worst mistakes investors make when buying mutual funds. Some of
these mistakes have been mentioned previously, but I think it is useful to enumerate them in one place. Consider this a checklist for novice
mutual fund investors and a reminder for more experienced ones.

1. *Not setting objectives.* You should never invest in a mutual fund, or
   anything else for that matter, until you have established your personal financial goals. If you don't know what you want to achieve,
   you can't possibly select the right funds for your needs.

2. *Failing to understand risk.* I've heard horror stories from conservative
   investors who plunged thousands of maturing GIC dollars into volatile
   funds, not comprehending the high risks involved. All mutual funds
   carry a degree of risk, but some are inherently more risky than others. Make sure you understand exactly what these risks are before you
   commit your money.

Many beginning mutual fund investors plunge in
# without getting solid advice.

3. *Failing to understand the relationship between interest rates and fixed income funds.* It's very simple. When interest rates rise, the unit value of bond and mortgage funds tends to decline. When rates fall, unit values rise. This is why fixed income funds produced high returns during the 1991–93 period and then gave back a big chunk of those gains in the first half of '94. But remember that even when unit values are declining, fixed income funds still generate interest income for you. As long as you don't panic and sell at a loss, you'll do all right over the long term.

4. *Getting hung up on performance ratings.* Past results are useful in assessing a mutual fund's consistency. But too many people base their investment decisions on history and nothing more. There are many other factors to consider including managerial changes, current economic conditions, political events, trend patterns (how well has the fund done lately?), interest rate movements, and cost.

5. *Not getting advice.* Many beginning mutual fund investors plunge in without getting solid advice. The proliferation of no-load funds through banks, trust companies, credit unions, and telephone order firms like Altamira has contributed to this trend. This isn't to say no-load funds are bad—far from it. But if you buy no-load funds without any clear under-

danger zone
**WATCH OUT FOR HYPE**

The novice investors who were hardest hit by switching from GICs into mutual funds in early 1994 were those who bought into the froth surrounding some of the hotter funds of the day. Latin American, emerging markets, and Far East funds all went through rough periods in the two years that followed. If you're a conservative investor who's trying mutual funds for the first time, stick with those that take a conservative approach.

standing of what you're doing, you may run into problems. If you're dealing with a financial institution, spend some time with a planning representative who knows what he or she is talking about (the level of expertise of such representatives can be spotty, so be careful). Or you can consult a fee-for-service financial planner, one who charges by the hour but doesn't sell product. The key point is that if you're not sure what you're doing, get help. Investment mistakes can be very expensive.

6. *Putting all your money in one place.* Diversification is one of the keys to investing success. In the case of mutual funds, this doesn't just mean distributing your assets among several funds. It also means using more than one fund group. Even though the funds within a group may be run by different managers, the managers usually talk to each other and often share similar investment philosophies. When they're wrong (it does happen) or out of sync with economic developments, the result can be below-average performance by many funds, not just one. This is what happened to Mackenzie Financial in the early '90s and it explains why all of their Industrial Canadian equity funds underperformed during this period. The solution is to select three solid mutual fund companies and distribute your assets among them. This way, if one falters, the other two may pick up the slack.

danger zone

## PANIC IN THE STREETS

An example of how lack of advice can lead to big losses occurred during the bond market free-fall of early 1994. Because of low interest rates, many investors had shifted maturing GIC money into fixed income mutual funds in late 1993 and early '94. When the value of bond fund units started to plunge in late winter, some people panicked and sold, locking in losses and souring them on mutual funds. Industry figures show that most sellers were investors in no-load bank funds. People with financial advisors were more likely to hold on and benefitted from the big bond market rally later in the year and into 1995.

trade talk

## RESOURCE FUND UPS AND DOWNS

The recent results of the Universal Canadian Resource Fund show how cyclical funds can fluctuate. In 1990 and 1991, when Canada was in a recession and resource companies were doing poorly, the fund recorded back-to-back losses of 19.9 percent and 12.5 percent. But in 1992 and 1993, the country turned the corner and started the climb back to prosperity. Resource stocks usually do well in such conditions and this fund responded accordingly, with annual gains of 35.8 percent and a whopping 89.2 percent. In retrospect, this would have been the time to bail out. The fund dropped 8.4 percent when markets went into a slide in 1994 and struggled through most of '95.

7. *Holding cyclical funds.* Most mutual funds should be purchased as long-term holds. A few should be actively traded. Cyclical funds—those that invest in sectors of the economy that are subject to boom and bust cycles—are classic examples of funds that should be sold when their upward move has about run its course. Natural resource funds are the most common type of cyclical fund in Canada.

8. *Failing to use asset allocation.* If the response to a question I asked at some of my seminars is a true indication, most Canadians missed out on the big bond market profits of 1991–93 and again on the big move in 1995. This obviously meant they weren't using asset allocation techniques, because if they had been, there would have been some bonds or bond funds in their portfolio. Proper asset mix is one of the most effective ways to reduce risk in a mutual fund portfolio while ensuring that at least a portion of your holdings will benefit from major upturns, whether in the stock market, the bond market, or interest rates.

9. *Being unrealistic.* Occasionally, a mutual fund will turn in an incredible one-year performance, gaining 50 percent or more. It's great when it happens. The problem is that bonanzas like this often create unrealistic expectations in the minds of investors, especially those without a great deal of mutual fund experience. Then when things revert to normal, as they inevitably do, disappointment sets in. Keep things in perspective. If your fund produces an average annual compound rate of return of between 10 and 15 percent over a decade, it's doing all right. If the return is over 15 percent, it's an outstanding performance.

trade talk

**ELUSIVE GOAL**

To illustrate how rare a feat it is, only three mutual funds sold in Canada managed an average annual return of more than 15 percent for the decade ending November 30, 1995. They were Bullock American (18.4 percent a year on average), Trimark Fund (15.5 percent), and C.I. Pacific (15.2 percent).

10. *Not diversifying geographically.* Canada is a small country economically, with limited industry and a volatile currency. Choosing only Canadian mutual funds therefore limits your profit potential and increases your risk. Hold at least a quarter of your mutual fund assets in non-Canadian funds.

# A manager's investment

style can tell you a great deal about a fund's likelihood to produce above-average returns and the amount of risk you're undertaking. . . . Value managers try to buy $1 worth of assets for 40¢—and often succeed. . . . Sector rotators can run into serious problems if the cycles don't move in the predicted patterns, as Mackenzie Financial found out. . . .

The deeper you go into mutual funds, the more you'll hear about managers' styles. This one is a value investor, that one is a sector rotator, this one is top down, that one is bottom up. It can all get somewhat technical and confusing, the more so because some managers refuse to be pigeon-holed, saying they use whatever approach works at the time. But if you really want to understand what's happening inside the mutual fund you're considering, you have to know the basic styles and what they mean in real terms.

The styles I'm about to describe all relate to equity funds. Fixed income managers also have their own styles, but they tend to be highly esoteric and little understood outside the tightly knit world of bond traders. With this caveat, here we go. We'll begin with the two basic management styles, top down and bottom up.

## TOP DOWN

This approach places the emphasis on markets and sectors, rather than on individual stocks. The top-down manager of a Canadian stock fund

## A TOP-DOWN MANAGER

James Blake, who runs the successful National Life Equities Fund, is a classic example of a top-down manager. First, he identifies which industry sectors he expects to outperform the market; then he selects companies that are leaders in their business and have solid fundamentals. His portfolio mainly consists of large companies, but some small ones are tossed into the mix for added growth potential. Results have been very good; for the five-year period to November 30, 1995, his fund returned an average of 12.5 percent a year.

will use an analysis of the current economic situation as a starting point. From there, he'll seek to identify those sectors of the economy that are likely to outperform under his most likely scenario. The fund's portfolio will be most heavily weighted to those sectors, and underweighted in areas the manager believes will do poorly. Once all this is done, the actual stocks are selected, usually from industry leaders in the most promising sectors.

For example, during the later stages of an economic recovery, resource stocks and consumer issues often do very well. Since interest rates are usually rising in this situation, utilities, which are highly interest-sensitive, may do badly. So a top-down manager who would normally give oil and gas stocks a 10 percent weighting in the fund's portfolio might increase this to 15 percent. Utilities stocks, which might normally get a 12 percent weighting, could be cut back to 8 percent.

Managers of top-down international funds take the same approach but do so on a country-by-country basis. A European fund manager, for example, might decide that Scandinavia, Britain, and Spain have above-average prospects for the coming year. Germany and France might be seen as below-average. She would then adjust her portfolio composition to reflect this view.

## BOTTOM UP

The true bottom-up manager isn't indifferent to what's happening in the economy, but he doesn't view it as the number one priority in stock selection. A bottom-up manager takes the position that what *really* matters is the quality of a company. If it's a well-managed firm with solid growth potential, then this fact will eventually be reflected in the share value.

Bottom-up managers are essentially fundamentalists. They spend much time analyzing company balance sheets, talking to managers, and visiting the plants or mining sites to see for themselves what's actually happening. In some ways, their approach is more difficult than that of a top-down manager because there's a higher degree of subjectivity involved. They must ask themselves questions such as these: Is that company president really telling me the full story? Is this sales team capable of cranking up revenues by 30 percent next year? Is the new capital expenditure going to pay off as quickly as the chief financial officer calculates?

The economy is tough enough to predict, although the broad trends tend to be fairly evident at any given time. The bottom-up manager goes beyond these, to make big bets on people and products—variables that are even more uncertain than the economic winds.

Top down and bottom up are basically different ways to select stocks. The next level of managerial styles gets

trade talk

### A BOTTOM-UP MANAGER

Tim McElvaine, who runs the Cundill Security Fund from his home near Kingston, Ontario, uses a bottom-up approach to stock picking. His emphasis is on seeking out companies with solid fundamentals that are trading at bargain prices. His efforts have turned around a fund that for years was an underachiever. The three-year average annual return to November 30, 1995 (which covers the period since McElvaine took over), was a terrific 21.5 percent.

more sophisticated, because it involves deciding what type of stocks will be chosen by the method being used. This is the level at which the character and the priorities of a mutual fund portfolio are established.

## The Intelligent Investor by Benjamin Graham is the bible of value managers.

### inside info

### BUYING BERKSHIRE

Berkshire Hathaway is the world's most expensive publicly traded stock. At the start of 1996, a single share was going for more than US$32,000, putting it well out of the range of most investors. But there's a much less expensive way to get in on the action. The Hamilton, Ontario-based AIC Value Fund holds about half its portfolio in Berkshire Hathaway shares or in companies that play a prominent role in the Berkshire portfolio, like Coca-Cola. Predictably, AIC's record has been very good—an average annual return of 22 percent for the five years to November 30, 1995. And you can buy in for just $500.

### VALUE

The bible of value managers is Benjamin Graham's classic stock selection guide, *The Intelligent Investor.* In it, he sets out the basic principles of value investing, which are directed at seeking out stocks that represent a combination of low risk and excellent value. Countless mutual fund portfolios have been built on these principles, some more successfully than others. Warren Buffett's fabled Berkshire Hathaway company in the U.S. (an investment firm) employs Graham's principles in its stock selection approach—buy cheap and hold forever, if possible.

The main drawback to value investing is the emphasis it places on buying out-of-favour stocks that are trading at below the company's break-up value and then waiting until the market recognizes the hidden gem and bids the price up to realistic levels. Sometimes this process can take a long time, so a fund that's built on value investing may not be the best choice for an investor seeking fast growth.

Some of the top value funds in Canada include those managed by the Trimark organization, the Cundill Value Fund, and the BPI Canadian Equity Value Fund, run by Steven Misener.

GROWTH

The growth manager doesn't really care whether a stock is selling at a bargain price. Her main interest is in how fast the value is likely to run up. So a growth portfolio will consist mainly of stocks of fast-growing companies with high earnings potential—hot stocks, if you like. You'll often find many small cap companies in a growth fund, because they offer the best opportunity for fast price movement.

trade talk

**SIR JOHN'S LEGACY**

The godfather of value investing in Canadian mutual funds is the legendary Sir John Templeton, who built a financial empire on searching out bargains all over the world. His original fund, Templeton Growth, has been churning out profits for more than 40 years (it was started in 1954 under the name Templeton Growth Fund of Canada). The Templeton organization delights in pointing out that if you'd invested $10,000 way back then, you'd be a multi-millionaire today.

## Templeton Growth Fund is one of the oldest value funds in Canada and one of the most successful.

As a result, growth portfolios are best suited for more aggressive investors seeking maximum capital appreciation. But be careful, because a growth-oriented fund may be more risky than one that's based on a value approach. The reason for this is that many of the stocks in the portfolio may trade at high multiples—prices well in excess of where they should be based on traditional ratios such as share price to profits (known as a price–earnings ratio). Investors often

## the fine print

**SMALL CAP**

Small cap companies are those that are just starting out or are relatively modest in size. The definition of what constitutes a small cap stock varies, but in Canada companies with market capitalization (the collective value of all outstanding stock) of under $150 million are usually considered to be in this class. In the U.S., a small cap company may have a market capitalization of up to US$500 million.

bid up values of quality growth shares in anticipation of future earnings increases. If they fail to materialize, the stock can drop in a big hurry. So growth-oriented funds may produce big gains when the manager gets it right, but be prepared for losses if things turn sour.

SPECULATIVE

At times it can be difficult to distinguish between a growth style and a speculative style, but some funds clearly fall into the latter category. A speculative approach involves investing in unproven stocks with little to go on but a good idea or a promising bit of territory to explore for minerals. A classic example of a speculative fund is the Vancouver-based Multiple Opportunities Fund, which warns in its prospectus that the managers will invest in "companies with no history of earnings, natural resource companies in the exploration and development stage, industrial companies in the start-up stage which are involved in the sale, manufacture or development of new products, and companies which are designated 'Venture Companies' on the Vancouver Stock Exchange." If this isn't enough to scare you off, the prospectus underlines the uncertainty attached to these stocks further on: "The business activities of junior natural resource companies are highly speculative and involve significant risk."

So why would anyone choose such a high-risk fund? Profits, that's why. Multiple Opportunities was the top-performing Canadian equity fund over the decade ending November 30, 1995, with an average annual return of 14.6

percent. But to get there, you had to have a strong stomach. The 51.4 percent loss the fund took in 1988 would have sent most investors scurrying for the exits.

## SECTOR ROTATION

This is the extension of the top-down investing approach carried to the next level. A sector rotation manager focuses primarily on cyclical companies—those that tend to perform especially strongly at certain points in the business cycle. The idea is to overweight the portfolio with stocks that are likely to do better than the market in general, thereby generating above-average returns for investors. Some of the favourite areas for this style of investing are automobile manufacturers, steel companies, forestry companies, mining firms, energy stocks, and airlines.

trade talk

**GOING FOR BIG GAINS**

Richard Driehaus, the U.S.-based manager of the 20/20 Aggressive Growth Fund, is regarded as one of North America's leading growth managers. He zeros in on small- and medium-sized companies he thinks have the potential to produce big returns, and so far investors who've gotten on board have done very well. The fund, which was started in 1993, produced an average annual return of 19.1 percent for the two years ending November 30, 1995.

During times when economic conditions are bad, the sector rotator overloads the portfolio with so-called defensive stocks—shares in companies that aren't as vulnerable to recessionary conditions. These might include utilities, pipelines, pharmaceutical companies, and banks.

A top sector rotator can produce outstanding returns for mutual fund investors. But there's a fair amount of guesswork involved in the process and timing is a critical factor. If a manager takes a big position in a certain sector too early, the result can be a prolonged period of indifferent returns.

This is what happened to the managers of Mackenzie Financial's Industrial Group of Funds in the early 1990s. With the country in recession and stock prices cheap, big

**SPECULATIVE FUNDS**

Few funds that use a speculative style are available in this country. One that does is the Special Opportunities Fund, run by the same people as Multiple Opportunities. It invests internationally but hasn't been nearly as successful as its VSE-oriented counterpart. The Friedberg Currency Fund, which invests in currency futures with varying degrees of success, also falls into the speculative category. Some of the funds offered by the Vancouver-based Sagit organization are on the cusp between the growth and speculative categories, as is the hot-shot Marathon Equity Fund, located in Toronto.

funds like Industrial Growth and Industrial Horizon began to build the resource sector of their portfolios in anticipation of big moves in these stocks once the economy improved. The problem was that it took much longer than expected. While investors gnashed their teeth and redemptions mounted, the Industrial funds suffered through three lean years. For example, Industrial Growth, once the largest equity fund in the country, posted a loss of 15 percent in 1990, a tiny, below-average gain of 2.3 percent in 1991, and a loss of 4.8 percent in 1992. The fund's asset base collapsed. In 1989 it had approached $1.8 billion; by 1992 it was down to $852 million. Unitholders and brokers became frantic; I can't recall a single seminar in 1992 when someone didn't ask about whether to stay in the Industrial funds or quit. Things got so bad that I devoted an entire chapter to the subject in my *1993 Buyer's Guide to Mutual Funds*, which came out in the late fall of 1992. In it, I wrote: "If you already own units in Industrial Growth and Industrial Horizon, my advice is to hold on. Having come this far, the worst thing you could do would be to sell and then watch the funds take off."

In 1993, Industrial Growth gained almost 47 percent, while Industrial Horizon advanced over 38 percent. The managers were finally vindicated, but it took a long time and

Mackenzie's reputation (and asset base) suffered severely in the process.

If you choose a sector rotation fund, be aware that this type of problem can arise. The biggest mistake is to become impatient and cash out just before the cycle moves.

### CAPITAL PROTECTION

This managerial style emphasizes the preservation of capital. High returns are sacrificed for the sake of maintaining a defensive portfolio that will provide decent profits in good times and keep losses to a minimum when things get rough.

There are a number of ways to achieve this end. Some managers rely heavily on computer programs to tell them when to get into and out of the markets. Some maintain high cash positions in difficult times to reduce a fund's volatility. Others use a variety of hedge instruments, like futures and options.

**trade talk**

**VARIED STYLES**

In an attempt to prevent a reoccurrence of the events of the early '90s, Mackenzie Financial now operates three distinct groups of funds, each with a dominant investing style. The Industrial Funds still rely heavily on sector rotation, although the managers insist they blend in other styles as well when appropriate. The Ivy Funds, managed by Gerald Coleman and Jerry Javasky, take a value-oriented approach. The Universal Funds, which employ a variety of managers, mainly use a growth style.

The track record of capital protection managers in Canada is somewhat mixed. One of the most successful managers in terms of results has been Jean-Pierre Fruchet, who runs a Toronto-based company called Guardian Timing Services. His flagship fund, the GTS Canadian Protected Fund, was started in late 1984 and uses portfolio insurance and market timing techniques to safeguard investors from losses. It's worked remarkably well: Over the eleven years from 1985 to 1995, the fund had only one losing year, when it dropped 1.5 percent in 1994. However,

 danger zone

## BOND BUST

A fund set up specifically to protect the capital base of fixed income investors sent its creators back to the drawing board after the system failed during the bond market drop of 1994. The Vancouver-based Top Fifty T-Bill/Bond Fund was supposed to keep investors out of harm's way by switching assets into T-bills when interest rates were on the rise and building bond holdings when rates were falling (and bond prices rising as a result). But somehow, the signals got crossed in '94. The unit value fell a whopping 9.3 percent during the year, placing the fund at position number 106 out of 110 bond funds surveyed by Southam's *Mutual Fund SourceBook* and proving once again that not all capital protection theories work out as well in practice as they do on paper.

even that negative result was much better than the average for that tough year.

The downside is that while the fund did its basic job of protecting capital, returns have been well below average. This may partly explain why, despite its success in fulfilling its mandate, the Canadian Protected Fund has never attracted much investor interest. Going into 1996, its asset base was only about $3 million.

### INDEXING

An index fund is one with a mandate to track a specific market index, such as the TSE 300. Its portfolio will be set up to reflect exactly the index it tracks. So returns will always approximate whatever the broader market does. You might call this the lazy person's style of mutual fund management. An index fund manager needs do little more than ensure his portfolio always reflects the index that it is supposed to mirror.

A number of index funds are available in Canada. Which you select depends on where you want to put your investing emphasis. For instance, a fund that tracks the TSE 300 will reflect the return of the broad Canadian market. But one that tracks the TSE 35 will focus on blue chip stocks. U.S. index funds may focus on the Dow Jones Industrial Average (blue chip), the Standard and Poor's 500 (broad market), or the NASDAQ index (mainly high-tech growth).

Which type of index fund you choose will make a big difference to your returns. The following table shows what happened to each of these key indexes in 1995. (The figures come from *The Globe and Mail*.)

| | |
|---|---|
| NASDAQ | +39.9% |
| S&P 500 | +34.1% |
| Dow Jones | +33.5% |
| TSE 300 | +11.9% |
| TSE 35 | +11.5% |

On the whole, index funds have not been particularly impressive performers in this country (although they've done better in the U.S.) Two of the oldest are the Great West Life Equity Index Fund and the Green Line Canadian Index Fund. Both posted returns that stood well below the average of Canadian equity funds as a group over the decade to the end of 1995.

The bottom line is that a manager's style can make a significant difference in your potential return and on the amount of risk you are undertaking. This is why it's important to establish what approach is being used to run the fund's portfolio *before* you invest any money. If the manager's style isn't consistent with what you're trying to achieve, look elsewhere.

# Many questionable sales

practices have been eliminated by the industry, but you still must be careful. . . . Watch out for cursory "financial plans," which are in fact just disguised sales promotions. . . . Discount brokers may save you money, but you could end up paying a fee to acquire supposed no-load funds. . . .

There's an old saying in this industry: "Mutual funds are sold, not bought." The implication is obvious: You, the investor, would never purchase a mutual fund were it not for the persistent efforts of an aggressive salesperson. Clearly, this kind of thinking is a throwback to the days when mutual funds were in disrepute, due to the machinations of some unscrupulous promoters. However, today's mutual fund industry is generally well run, reasonably well regulated, and offers a wide variety of legitimate investment options.

Most of the industry's more questionable sales practices were addressed in late 1995 when the Investment Funds Institute of Canada issued a Code of Sales Practices for member companies. The code dealt with many of the issues that had been raised in a report prepared earlier in the year for the Ontario Securities Commission by Glorianne Stromberg. In it, she was critical of certain practices that could possibly work against the best interests of an investor. Most of the changes in the way mutual funds are sold dealt with potential conflict of interest situations that might influence a salesperson to recommend funds that were not appropriate for the investor. Some examples:

Free trips: In the past, some fund companies sponsored "educational" trips to exotic locales for big sales producers. They can still have the trips, but the sponsors can no longer pay travel and accommodation costs, which virtually eliminates them as an incentive.

Tiered fees: Some companies paid a higher commission rate when certain sales levels were met. This could influence a sales rep who was close to the magic level to push funds from a certain group.

Loans and advances: One big fund group got into trouble with regulators over large loans made to a sales organization. The concern was that the distributor might tend to favour funds from the lending organization as a result. The new Code of Sales prohibits this practice.

As a result, the mutual fund sales arena is much cleaner. However, there are still many things to be careful about when buying fund units. Further on, you'll find some tips that may help you negotiate the sales jungle effectively. But first let's look at the various people with whom you'll be dealing when you make your purchase. They include:

### STOCKBROKERS

Mutual funds have become one of the main products for retail brokers, especially with small investors who are nervous about the stock market but want to put their money in something more exciting than GICs. As a result, many brokers have made it a point to become quite knowledgable about the major fund companies. For the most part, however, it's been a self-education process because most brokerage firms still do not employ mutual fund analysts to provide guidance (Nesbitt Burns is one of the few exceptions). As a result, most brokers are only familiar with the funds of a half-dozen companies at most. Ask them about more obscure funds and they'll either try to bluff it or admit they don't know and say they'll get back to you. If recommendations and insights are important to you (which they should be if you're paying a broker's commission), this makes buying funds this way a hit or miss proposition. Protect yourself by doing your own research in advance and probing the broker's knowledge about the funds that interest you. If he or she can't tell you anything you don't already know, consider taking your business to a discount broker and paying less commission. One other disadvantage of buying through brokers is that unless you're a very good client, they'll be reluctant to acquire no-load funds for you.

### DISCOUNT BROKERS

Most of the major banks now offer a discount brokerage service. Green Line, operated by Toronto-Dominion Bank, is the largest and best known. But if you aren't a regular TD customer, you may wish to ask if your own bank offers a similar service before opening a Green Line account. Compare the fees and the convenience factor before deciding. You can often (but not always) acquire mutual funds through a discount broker at a lower commission than you'd pay a full-service broker. However, don't expect any advice—discount brokers basically take orders only. And be aware that if you place an order for a no-load fund through a discount broker, there will usually be a commission involved. In most cases, this is imposed when the units are sold.

### FINANCIAL PLANNERS

Many financial planners also double as sales reps. You should be aware of this when you consult them. A planner who operates strictly on a fee-for-service basis and is not interested in selling you anything can be relied on for unbiased advice. However, if the planner stands to benefit if you follow her recommendations—for example, by purchasing a specific mutual fund—you should be aware of this. Ask the planner up front how she is compensated. The advantage of good financial planners is that they'll prepare a detailed mutual fund investment program for you and construct a portfolio that's suited to your needs (brokers will rarely perform this time-consuming service). The disadvantage is that, as with brokers, financial planners who are compensated through commissions may not be keen to add no-load funds to your mix, although some will do it as a service.

 danger zone

**FAKE PLANS**

Some salespeople will offer a free "financial plan" as an inducement. It may be legitimate, or it may be designed primarily to persuade you to invest heavily in one or more of their funds. If you're suspicious about the plan you receive, ask some tough questions. It may just be a sales promotion gimmick; if so, don't let it influence your buying decision.

### MUTUAL FUND BROKERS

These are people who specialize in mutual fund sales only. Typically, they offer funds from a number of firms and will work with you to find the ones best suited to your needs. In most cases, however, they will not offer the traditional type of no-load fund. Their commissions will be similar to those charged by full-service brokers and financial planners. However, they probably won't prepare a full-scale plan for you.

### COMPANY SALES REPS

Some companies employ their own salespeople to promote and sell their funds. Investors Group typifies this sales approach. In the past, Investors Group reps offered only their own fund line, but competitive pressures have forced the company to expand their product range greatly.

### INSURANCE SALESPEOPLE

The insurance industry offers its own type of mutual funds, known as segregated funds (see chapter 17 for more details). These funds are often, but not always, tied in to some form of insurance contract. They're sold by agents and brokers representing the specific companies. The major disadvantage of buying funds in this way is that commissions may be higher than for ordinary mutual funds and are normally not negotiable.

### FINANCIAL INSTITUTIONS

Most banks and trust companies offer their own line of mutual funds, usually no-load. A few large credit unions also have one or more funds. Some of these fund groups have excellent performance records and switching is free. However, you may find that the mutual fund sales representative you deal with has a limited knowledge of the field and can only offer you very basic advice. The banks have undertaken expensive staff training programs to bring their reps up to speed, but staffing every branch with an expert is expensive and turnover is high. However, the banks have clearly recognized the immense profit potential in

*danger zone* ⚠️

**DOES THE BAY SEND YOU TO EATON'S?**

Although banks are moving into selling outside funds, they're not likely to praise the virtues of direct competitors. Scotiabank may offer a terrific line of funds, but don't expect a Royal Bank employee to let you in on this.

the distribution system they offer. Early in 1996, TD Bank received permission to sell a full range of mutual funds through its branch network, a move that may lead to other banks following suit.

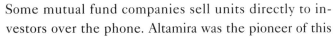

# TD is the first bank to offer a broad range of mutual funds (including load funds) through its branch network.

### FUND MANAGERS

Some mutual fund companies sell units directly to investors over the phone. Altamira was the pioneer of this type of marketing in Canada, but several other firms now offer the service, including the U.S.-based Scudder organization, which launched a Canadian operation in 1995. Funds sold in this way are usually no load, although there may be some other fees involved. For instance, Altamira charges a one-time fee to set up a new account.

So much for the people you'll be dealing with along the way. Now here are those buying tips that I promised.

1. *Negotiate all commissions.* Treat the mutual fund marketplace as you would a Mexican street vendor. Negotiate for the best possible price. Mutual fund companies authorize a range for commissions that may be charged for their products. In some cases, front-end loads can run as high as 9 percent.

### the fine print

**INFORMATION PLEASE**

Don't be surprised when a fund company representative starts asking what seem like very personal questions when you first phone to place an order. All mutual fund sales organizations are required by securities regulators to "know [their] client." The idea is to ensure that any recommendations are consistent with the investor's objectives and financial position. So don't be offended when you're asked about your goals, your job, and your income. It's part of the process. The only way to avoid it is not to invest.

Never pay this much. Discount brokers will charge 2–2.5 percent (they'll go as low as 1 percent on large orders). Full-service brokers and financial planners will want 3–4 percent. Here again, if your order is large, you may be able to get rates that are even lower. Also, remember that some back-end loads are now also negotiable. Ask before you commit.

2. *Negotiate sweeteners.* Mutual fund salespeople want your business. Every purchase of a load fund means an immediate commission for them, plus an on-going trailer fee to compensate them for continuing to service your account. As a result, they're often willing to toss in extras to attract you. Ask for no-fee switching and commission-free money market fund purchases for starters.

inside info

## HOW TO PAY NOTHING AT ALL

Some brokers will sell you a front-end load fund with no sales commission at all. Reason: although they give up the immediate payment, they'll continue to collect trailer fees for as long as you own your units. If their sales volume is high enough, they can live very comfortably on just trailer fee income. A few small companies have sprung up that sell mutual funds only in this way.

3. *Find out what the management fees are.* Before making a decision on whether to buy a front-end, back-end, or no-load fund, ask what the management fees are in each case. You'll often find that back-end and no-load purchase options carry a higher management fee, which will eat into your returns over time.

4. *Don't base your purchase decision on commission only.* Buying a no-load fund just as a means of saving the sales commission can be penny-wise and pound-foolish. There are many good no-load funds available, but there are also many mediocre and poor ones. Choose your funds on the basis of quality and their compatibility with your objectives.

5. *Arm yourself with knowledge.* As with any other purchase, if you set out to buy mutual funds without doing any homework, you'll be a sitting duck for any plausible sales pitch you encounter. Have some idea of what you want and why before you make contact with a salesperson. If he recommends something else instead, ask him to explain why his suggestion is superior to your original choice.

6. *Don't Pay MMF Commissions.* As a general rule, you should never pay a commission of any kind on the purchase of a money market fund. Some companies post maximum rates of 2 percent (a few are even higher). But if anyone actually tries to charge you this amount, resist. Returns on these funds usually aren't high enough to justify a commission fee of any kind. There are many excellent no-load money market funds around; choose one of them if the sales rep insists on a commission.

# Segregated funds offer

some unique advantages, such as a guarantee you won't lose any money. . . . High sales commissions and management fees are among the drawbacks to buying these funds in some cases. . . . Check the performance records closely. Some segregated funds are chronic underachievers. . . .

Life insurance companies have their own version of mutual funds, which are generically known as *segregated funds* which simply means a fund's assets are held separately, or segregated, from the other assets of the insurance company. It's an awful term—certainly no marketing expert coined it. Just because the name is unattractive, though, doesn't mean you should overlook these vehicles. In some cases, they might be exactly what you require.

The difference between these funds and other mutual funds is more than a technical matter of how the investments are held. Segregated funds are unlike those you purchase through mutual fund companies, financial institutions, financial planners, or brokers in several ways. They offer advantages not available with other funds, but they have disadvantages as well.

The three unique advantages to segregated funds that do not apply to ordinary mutual funds are:

## GUARANTEES

With an ordinary mutual fund, your investment is totally at risk. Mutual funds are not protected by deposit insurance and fund managers take pains to point out that a strong past performance record is no guarantee of future results. If a fund makes poor investments, the value of the assets it holds will decline and so will the value of your units. But with segregated funds, you have a degree of protection. Some insurance companies guarantee that at maturity of the investment contract or at death, you or your estate will receive not less than 75 percent of the total amount you invested in the fund over the years. Other companies, looking for a competitive edge, offer a guarantee equal to 100 percent of your invested cash. This is a no-loss guarantee, even if the stock market goes through the floor. Of course, if the investment climate got that bad, you'd have to wonder whether the company would still be around to honour the guarantee.

## danger zone
## NO PROFIT GUARANTEE

A guarantee may look attractive at first glance; remember, though, that even with a 100 percent guarantee, you'll receive no return on your investment if it has to be invoked. You'll get back your original stake, but your money won't have earned anything during the years it was invested with the company. Still, many people like the idea of placing a limit on their potential losses, especially if they're investing in equity funds. A guarantee provides this.

CREDITOR PROTECTION

If a close family member is named as beneficiary, segregated funds offer a degree of protection for your investments in the event that you run into financial problems and have to declare bankruptcy. However, recent court rulings have indicated this protection may not be absolute and may not apply in some cases. If this is important to you, get legal advice.

ESTATE PLANNING

Assets in a segregated fund pass directly to the beneficiary if you die. This means they avoid probate fees, which are on the rise in some provinces. Also, assets in segregated funds may receive favourable tax treatment if the investment is being made as part of a life insurance contract. In such a case, when you die, no capital gains tax is payable on the profits. Your beneficiary inherits the money tax-free, as part of the life insurance proceeds.

These are the pluses of segregated funds. Before you get too excited about them, consider their disadvantages.

### LACK OF FLEXIBILITY

Because segregated funds are usually used as a method of saving for an insurance or retirement annuity contract, a penalty may be imposed if you want to cash out early. This isn't always true, however; many companies will allow you to cash your units at any time, just as you can with a regular mutual fund. Since policies vary from one company to another, make appropriate inquiries.

### FORCED CONTRIBUTIONS

Some segregated funds can only be purchased through an investment contract with the insurance company that requires you put in a certain amount of money each month ("minimum premium" is the insurance terminology). A minimum monthly premium of $50 is typical, unless you're prepared to invest at least $1,000 up front. In some cases, these premiums may be waived in the event that you become disabled.

### HIGH COMMISSIONS

Sales commissions for segregated funds can sometimes be high and, unlike commissions for ordinary funds, they are

the fine print

## HIGH FEES

Here are some examples of segregated funds that charge management fees that I consider to be out of line. In some cases, the charges are so excessive as to be almost usurious; one blatant example is the money market fund from Manulife.

| Fund | Management Expense Ratio* |
|---|---|
| Empire Elite Equity | 2.57% |
| Great-West Life Canadian Bond | 2.40% |
| Great-West Life Canadian Equity | 2.64% |
| Great-West Life Mortgage | 2.40% |
| Maritime Life Money Market Fund | 1.75% |
| Manulife VistaFund Short-Term Securities 2 | 2.38% |

\* As reported by *The Globe and Mail*, January 18, 1996.

usually non-negotiable. Rates will vary from one company to another, so ask.

### HIGH MANAGEMENT FEES

Some segregated funds are assessed unconscionably high management fees, thus reducing investor returns. In some cases, these fees are totally out of line with the industry in general. But note that this criticism doesn't apply to all insurance companies. Several have kept their fees at reasonable levels; you'll have to search them out. Also, it should be noted that in some cases the management expense ratio is high because the funds themselves are quite small. Since some expenses are fixed, a smaller fund will be charged a higher amount in percentage terms. So a $500,000 expenditure on a computer system will have a bigger proportionate impact on a $10-million fund than on a $500-million one.

### POOR PRODUCT CHOICE

There is no family of segregated funds that comes close to matching the major mutual fund companies in terms of the variety of products they offer. For example, if you want to invest in a Far East fund, you'll find only two insurance companies (Maritime Life and NN) that include such an option in their segregated fund line. Also, in practical terms you're limited to the funds offered by one particular group.

London Life may have the best mortgage fund and National Life the best Canadian stock fund, but you won't be able to put both in the same portfolio.

## SPOTTY PERFORMANCE

Some segregated fund groups have an excellent performance record. The funds offered by National Life are an example. Others, such as those from Metropolitan Life, are chronic underachievers. You'll need to be very selective.

## LACK OF INFORMATION

Details about segregated funds can sometimes be difficult to obtain. When researching various books, I often found that when I called certain insurance companies to ask for material about their funds, it was difficult to find someone who knew about them. This appears to be because insurance companies are often very large and segregated funds represent a small part of their business. Whatever the reason, it can be frustrating to a potential buyer.

## SALESPEOPLE

Buying units in a segregated fund will get a life insurance salesperson on your case. Remember, this is the main business of the company. Since you've already decided to do business with them, you've become a hot prospect.

If you want to invest in segregated funds, be prepared to do extensive research first. There are advantages to doing so, but, as with other insurance products, trying to sort through the various funds and choose the best ones isn't always easy.

One other key point. Although the funds offered directly by life insurance companies are segregated funds, those available through subsidiary or affiliated companies may not be. In such cases, you will not receive the guarantees associated with segregated funds.

# The **Mutual Group of Funds** is controlled by Mutual Life, but they are not segregated funds.

So you may be offered a fund, which, at first glance, appears to be a segregated fund because it bears the name of an insurance company. On closer examination, however, you may find that it's just an ordinary mutual fund, offered by a subsidiary of a life insurance firm. An example is the Mutual Group of Funds. They are administered by Mutual Diversico Inc., managed by Mu-Canada Investment Counselling Ltd., sold by Mutual Investco Inc., with the Mutual Trust Company acting as trustee. All these firms are effectively controlled by Mutual Life. But Mutual Life does not manage or sell these funds directly and they are not segregated funds.

# Closed-end funds usually

trade at a discount, but this doesn't mean you can't make money from them. . . . Don't buy closed-end funds on the initial offering. You'll usually get a better price if you wait. . . . REITs are a specialized form of closed-end fund that are one of the best-kept tax shelter secrets in Canada. . . .

Just when you think you know everything about mutual funds, someone comes along and does it a little differently. This is the case with closed-end funds. Think of them as a hybrid, a cross between a mutual fund and a stock. These funds can sometimes offer unexpected profit potential. So you need to understand how they work and when to take advantage of them.

Most of the mutual funds you'll encounter are structured as open-end funds. This means there is no limit on the number of units they can distribute. Whenever an investor wants to buy in, the fund simply issues new units from its treasury at the current net asset value (NAV). In this way, the issuing of new units does not reduce the value of those currently outstanding (a process known technically as "dilution"). In the case of the Pape Fund, if someone bought 10 new units, the fund would end up with an additional $1,000 in assets from the cash acquired as a result of the sale (assuming no sales commissions are involved). So it would now have $101,000 in assets and 1,010 units outstanding. The NAV per unit would remain unchanged at $100.

## NET ASSET VALUE

The net asset value of a fund unit is calculated by dividing the net assets of the fund (the market value of all holdings less any liabilities) by the number of units outstanding at any given time. So, for example, if the Pape Fund had $100,000 in net assets and there were 1,000 units outstanding, the NAV of each unit would be $100. If it's an open-end fund, this is the price a new investor would pay to acquire units.

An open-end fund will also redeem your units at the current NAV, usually with minimal notice. Again, there is no impact on the NAV of other unitholders when this happens; the purchase process is simply reversed. For instance, if you wanted to redeem 50 units of the Pape Fund, you would notify the company through your sales representative. They would issue you a cheque for $5,000 (50 units multiplied by the current $100 NAV). The fund would then be left with assets of $95,000 and a total of 950 units outstanding. The NAV remains at $100.

The only way the NAV changes in an open-end fund is if the value of the underlying assets change. Suppose, for example, that the Pape Fund received dividends of $3,000 from stocks it holds. Total assets of the fund therefore increase to $103,000. The 100 units outstanding now have a net asset value of $103 each, which represents a 3 percent increase in their worth. If the fund distributes these dividends to its unitholders by issuing cheques, then the net assets of the fund will again be worth $100,000 and the NAV will be back to $100—but you'll have received a dividend of $3 per unit to compensate for the drop.

The overwhelming majority of mutual funds sold in Canada are the open-end type. But you may occasionally be offered an opportunity to buy into a closed-end fund. These funds issue a limited number of units. When the issue is fully subscribed, the offer is closed. No more units are made available at that time, although there may be additional offerings in the future.

This means if you want to buy units in a closed-end fund once the initial offering period is over, you have to find someone willing to sell them to you. To facilitate the process, units in most closed-end funds are listed on a stock exchange, where they can be bought and sold more easily. You'll find several closed-end funds traded on the Toronto Stock Exchange—examples include the New Altamira Value Fund, BGR Precious Metals Fund, First Australia Prime Income Fund, and Central Fund.

Unlike open-end funds, the NAV is not the determining factor in the selling price of a closed-end fund's units (or shares). The price is set by the market, and often the market decides a closed-end fund should sell for less than its underlying NAV. When this happens, a closed-end fund is said to be trading at a discount. Most Canadian closed-end funds trade at a substantial discount to their NAV—occasionally over 30 percent. When this occurs, you are essentially buying a dollar's worth of assets for less than 70 cents.

**trade talk**

## NAV CALCULATIONS

Most open-end mutual funds calculate their NAV on a daily basis. However, some do it weekly and a few (usually real estate funds) make the calculation only once a month. In the case of funds that evaluate their NAV less frequently, you're usually required to give longer notice if you want to redeem your units; some real estate funds may require you to wait up to 30 days or even longer (several actually suspended redemptions in the early '90s to avoid having to sell properties at distressed prices to raise cash). You can find the current NAV of all Canadian mutual funds in the business pages of most major newspapers or in the financial press.

At the beginning of 1996, for example, there were about 20 closed-end funds publicly traded in Canada. Of these, all but one were priced below their underlying net asset value. The deepest discount was in the Health Care and Biotechnology Fund, which was trading at $6.75. This was

## trade talk

### WHERE TO LOOK

Most Canadian closed-end funds are valued weekly and their current NAVs are published in the Saturday editions of *The Globe and Mail*'s "Report on Business" and *The Financial Post* in a box headed "Closed-End Funds." The *Post* also shows you the current relation between the fund's market price and its net asset value, which is essential information if you're investing in these funds.

39 percent below its NAV of $11.04. The only fund trading at a premium was First Australia Prime Income, a fund specializing in bonds and other debt securities from Australia and New Zealand. The premium was tiny, however—only 2.6 percent.

The reasons for the tendency of closed-end funds to trade at a discount are complex, but what it really comes down to is that the market penalizes these shares for their lack of flexibility and liquidity.

The situation is different in the U.S., where closed-end mutual funds are quite popular, especially with internationally minded people who want a stake in countries that are difficult to invest in directly. Hot funds traded on the New York Stock Exchange can sometimes carry very substantial premiums if investors expect their assets to rise rapidly in value. So closed-end funds don't always trade at a discount. But if they move to a high premium for any reason, you should probably sell. Sooner or later, investors will decide it's not worthwhile paying $1.25 for a dollar's worth of assets.

One important implication in all this for Canadian investors is not to buy a closed-end fund when it's initially offered unless there is some compelling reason to do so—for example, if the fund guarantees it will buy back your units at not less than issue price. Without such guarantees (which are virtually non-existent because they'd defeat one of the main advantages of a closed-end fund from the manager's perspective) the market value of the fund will usually drop once the issue is completed and shares start trading on a stock exchange. If you like the concept of the fund, you'll probably be able to buy units more cheaply at this time.

In recent years, two new closed-end funds attempted to break this cycle by offering sweeteners designed to keep their share price near or above the NAV. The first to appear was the New Altamira Value Fund, which had its initial public offering (IPO) in late 1993. The Templeton organization followed quickly on their heels with one of their own.

trade talk

## MANAGERS LOVE THEM

Altamira is a highly successful company that sells quality no-load mutual funds over the phone. It's been a thorn in the side of brokers and financial planners, who have seen millions of potential commission dollars flow away from them and into Altamira's coffers. In an effort to tap into some of this money, the brokerage community persuaded Altamira to produce a product they could sell to their clients, a classic example of the "if-you-can't-beat-'em-join-'em" philosophy. The result was the closed-end Value Fund, which was launched with a blue-ribbon distri-

If closed-end funds usually trade at a discount, why does anyone bother with them? The simple answer seems to be that fund managers love them. They always know exactly how much money they have available— since investors can't sell units back to the treasury, there's no need to keep large cash reserves. And the managers will never be placed in the position of having to sell assets in a down market because of a rash of redemptions.

bution team that included Richardson Greenshields, Midland Walwyn, RBC Dominion Securities, Wood Gundy, First Marathon, and Toronto-Dominion's Green Line. In Canadian financial terms, it represented the equivalent of North and South Korea signing a peace agreement.

But, like all other new closed-end fund issues, the promoters had to deal with the discount problem. How do you persuade investors to buy on the initial public offering when shares are probably going to sell at a discount once trading starts on the TSE?

Altamira and the underwriters came up with two devices to support the trading price. One was a time limit on the fund's life. It will automatically terminate in 2001, at which time the assets will be distributed to shareholders. The idea is that as the wind-up date approaches, the trading price of the shares will rise (or fall) to approach the net asset value.

The second, and potentially more potent, technique was a dividend reinvestment plan. The fund will pass through all profits to shareholders at least once a year. Investors who so wish can use these payments to acquire additional shares. If the stock price is less than the NAV at the time the share purchase plan cuts in, the additional units will be acquired by buying on the TSE. This will have the effect of supporting the market price. If shares are trading on the TSE at a premium to the market price, new units will be issued from the treasury.

When the shares began trading, the plan seemed to work. In early January 1994, shares were going at a 5 percent premium to net asset value. But then the old discount pattern took hold. The trading price dipped below the NAV and kept falling. By June of that year, you could buy shares at a discount of 15 percent to NAV—a great value for new buyers, but not so great if you had bought on the IPO.

The Templeton Emerging Markets Appreciation Fund was launched in June 1994 and offered the same type of dividend reinvestment plan as the Altamira fund. Another

**inside info**

**WATCH THE PATTERN**

Despite all the sweeteners, the Altamira fund has continued to trade at a discount most of the time, although the percentage varies considerably. At the beginning of 1996, the discount to NAV was 4.3 percent. If the discount slips to 10 percent or more, it should be treated as a buy signal.

inducement was a provision that the full subscription fee of $15 a unit would go directly into the fund—all sales commissions were paid by the Templeton Limited Partnership. This represented a break from past experience with closed-end funds and was intended to buoy up the market price.

Also, the Canadian fund was designed to mirror one that already traded on the New York Stock Exchange, usually at a premium. The investment community maintained that this would tend to keep the TSE price close to NAV levels.

In the beginning, the strategy worked—the fund regularly traded at close to its NAV, buoyed by investor excitement about the new world of emerging markets. But then the Mexican peso collapsed at the end of 1994 and the emerging markets balloon exploded. Money fled back into safer havens, with U.S. stocks among the major beneficiaries. Shares in the Templeton fund joined the deep discount parade. At the beginning of 1996, they were trading at 17.3 percent below the underlying asset value.

inside info

**A WINNING STRATEGY**

One potential bargain-hunting strategy is to buy shares of the Altamira and Templeton funds when they're at a deep discount and hold on until the annual reinvestment period. As the funds acquire new shares on the market, prices will tend to rise and you should be able to sell at a profit.

# The key to profiting from closed-end funds
## is to remember that they will usually trade at a discount.

The key to profiting from closed-end funds in Canada is always to remember that they will normally trade at a discount. It's the depth of the discount that offers the greatest opportunities. So be on the watch for potential profits when a discount becomes unrealistically large. There are several possible strategies:

*Bargain hunting* Investors see shares in the fund are trading at a low price relative to the fund's assets. For example, suppose the net asset value of shares in the High Flyers closed-end fund is $10 but they're trading for only $6 on the TSE—a 40 percent discount. Bargain hunters may bid up the price to $7, reducing the discount to 30 percent. If you bought in at $6, you'd make a quick profit of almost 17 percent in this situation.

*Range watching* Many closed-end funds trade within a predictable range—say, a 25 to 35 percent discount to NAV. Astute investors keep track of the price movements and buy when shares are trading in the low end of the range. When the price moves back to the high end, they sell and wait for the cycle to repeat.

*Fund wind-up* When a closed-end fund is wound up, all outstanding shares are redeemed at the final net asset value. Anyone who bought in at a discount stands to make a profit in this situation.

There are two kinds of wind-ups:

Maturity-based—When the fund is launched, a date is set for its wind-up, as we saw in the case of the Altamira fund. The process is an orderly one and the trading price of shares will gradually rise (or fall) towards the NAV as the wind-up date approaches.

Forced—Shareowners force the wind-up of the fund by special resolution. This is happening more frequently when shares consistently trade at a deep discount to NAV; by forcing liquidation, the shareowners are able to recover the full asset value of their holdings. Forced liquidations are unpredictable and, as a result, can produce windfall profits for investors who buy in at low prices.

*Conversion* A fourth way to realize quick profits from a closed-end fund is as a result of conversion to open-end status. This has happened more frequently in recent years as shareowners, unhappy with low stock exchange prices, approve special resolutions converting what was originally a closed-end fund to open-end status. This enables shareholders to redeem their units at net asset value, rather than being forced to sell them on a stock exchange at a discount.

One recent example of a forced conversion from a closed- to an open-end fund involved shareholders in the Germany Fund of Canada. The $127-million fund was started in 1990, at the height of investor enthusiasm over the collapse of the Iron Curtain and the reunification of Germany. It was well managed by the brokerage firm of McLean McCarthy, but consistently traded at a discount to NAV.

By early 1994, some large investors were fed up with the situation and moved to call a special meeting of shareholders with the aim of winding up the fund. At the time, units were trading at a discount to NAV of about 11 percent; winding up the fund would have allowed investors to recoup the full value.

In the end, it was decided to keep the fund going but to convert it to an open-end fund, managed by AGF. As far as investors were concerned, the effect was the same: the unit value rose to the true NAV and they were able to realize gains as a result.

A special category of closed-end fund is the real estate investment trust (REIT). Here the rules of the game are somewhat different—the profits come mainly from tax-advantaged cash flow.

inside info

**BEATING REVENUE CANADA**

The tax-sheltering effect of a REIT can be dramatic. In 1994, for example, less than 10 percent of the income paid to unitholders by RealFund was taxable. If you held 1,000 units of the fund, you would have received $1,080 in income that year. A top-bracket taxpayer would have been assessed only about $50 on this amount. But a word of warning: if you sell your units in the future, some of this unpaid tax will be snatched back through a complicated formula. Don't sell and you'll be okay.

## A special category of closed-end fund is the real estate investment trust (REIT).

There were four REITs in Canada at the beginning of 1996, the biggest being RealFund. All began as open-end funds but were forced to convert to closed-end status when the real estate crash of the early '90s produced a flood of redemption requests which could only be satisfied by selling off properties at fire sale prices. To protect unitholders who wanted to stay in, the funds converted to closed-end status. This enabled those who wanted to get out to sell their units on the Toronto Stock Exchange without forcing fund managers to put their properties up for sale under impossible market conditions.

REITs invest in commercial properties, such as shopping malls, office buildings, and medical centres. Their main source of income is the rent they generate. Profits are distributed to unitholders and are partially tax sheltered through the use of capital cost allowance (CCA).

REITs were slow to gain favour with investors because of the bad memories that lingered from the real estate crash. As a result, they have tended to trade at bargain prices relative to the tax-sheltered income they generate. To see if this is still the case, ask about the current price and look at the distributions made over the past year and the amount forecast for next year (a broker can get this information for you). Then ask how much of the distribution is likely to be tax free. If the numbers look good, you may have found another closed-end bargain. There are good profits to be made from trading in closed-end funds. You just have to know what you're doing.

# If you make money from

your mutual funds, Revenue Canada will want a share—but there are ways to reduce the tax bite. . . . Certain types of mutual fund distributions attract much less tax than others. . . . Labour-sponsored funds offer huge tax savings, but you must be willing to accept the risks involved. . . .

Unfortunately, there's no escape. As soon as you start making money in mutual funds, Revenue Canada will be there with its hand out, wanting its share. The trick is to give them as little as possible, while keeping them off your back. That's what this chapter is all about.

The only way to avoid giving the government a share of your profits each year is to hold your mutual funds in some type of registered plan: an RRSP, RRIF, Life Income Fund, or pension plan. You'll have to pay down the road, when you start drawing retirement income from your plan, but in the meantime the profits can compound tax free.

Any funds held outside a registered plan will be subject to tax each year. The rules can be somewhat complex, so here's a summary of the various ways in which Revenue Canada may come at you.

### DISTRIBUTIONS

Many mutual funds make periodic income distributions to their unitholders. In most cases, this is done once a year but some funds make distributions quarterly or even monthly. These distributions are considered to be taxable income in your hands (unless they're inside a registered plan) and must be declared each year on your return. You'll receive a tax slip from the fund company before the end of February each year, providing all the details that you need to complete your return. Distributions can take several forms, each of which may be taxed differently. They include:

Capital gains   This is your share of the profits realized by the fund from the sale of securities in the portfolio during the year. This form of distribution is taxed at the capital gains rate, which means the first 25 percent is tax free. You pay at your marginal rate on the balance.

Dividends   This distribution is your share of all dividends earned by the fund during the year. These payments are eligible for the dividend tax credit, so they'll be taxed at an advantageous rate. Dividends are one of the most effective ways to receive investment income in this country; the tax rate on them is actually lower than on capital gains.

Foreign income   If you own an international mutual fund, it may have received income from a number of foreign sources, including interest and dividends. The distribution is your share. If the fund paid tax on this money to other governments, you can recover some of this through the foreign tax credit.

the fine print

**MARGINAL TAX RATE**

Your marginal tax rate is the rate that applies on the last dollar you earn. Since we have a graduated tax system, your marginal rate increases as your income climbs. The highest marginal rate in Canada in 1995 was in British Columbia, where a resident paid 54.2 percent tax on every dollar earned after taxable income exceeded $78,202.

Other income   This usually refers to your share of any interest income earned by the fund. Interest doesn't receive any tax break, so you'll pay at your full rate.

Re-investments   Most mutual funds offer an automatic reinvestment program in which your distributions are used to buy more fund units. If you join, you won't actually receive any cash in your hands. But beware: as far as Revenue Canada is concerned, this money is still taxable, even though you never see it.

Rental income   These distributions come from real estate mutual funds and real estate investment trusts (REITs). They receive a special tax treatment because the fund managers normally use capital cost allowance (CCA) to shelter a large portion of the distribution from tax. You'll receive a special form for reporting this type of distribution on your return.

## SALES

Whenever you sell mutual fund units, a taxable transaction takes place. If you sell your units for more than you paid for them, you've earned a capital gain and will have to declare it for tax purposes. If you sell for less than you paid, you have a capital loss and you may be able to claim some tax relief.

Revenue Canada casts a very long shadow here. Transactions that you may not consider to constitute a sale will be viewed as such by the tax department and it will want a piece of the action. Some examples:

**Switches** When you move money from one fund to another, Revenue Canada regards the switch as two transactions: a sale and a purchase. If you've made a profit, the sale will trigger a tax liability.

**RRSP contributions** If you have a self-directed RRSP, you're allowed to contribute securities directly to it, instead of converting them to cash first. But the government regards such "contributions in kind" as a sale and you'll have to

danger zone

**DON'T OVERPAY!**

Some investors have paid too much tax on rental income distributions due to poor reporting procedures by brokerage houses. Because REITs are a relatively new investment form in Canada, there have been cases where brokers who hold units in accounts on behalf of clients have classified the distributions as dividends rather than rental income. The result is an enormous difference in tax payable. For example, a top-bracket Ontario resident should have paid only $53.08 in tax on the 1994 distribution from 1,000 shares of RealFund. But if this income was incorrectly reported as dividends (which happened in some cases), the tax bill soared to $387.94.

pay tax on any profits. The bad news is that if your fund units are on the losing end when you make this type of move, you cannot claim a capital loss.

Gifts   If you give your fund units to someone else (perhaps your spouse), this is considered to be a sale for tax purposes and you must declare any profits.

Death   You won't have to worry about it personally, but if you die your estate will have to deal with the fact that Revenue Canada will deem that all your mutual fund assets (and everything else) have been sold and any capital gains realized for tax purposes. The one exception is if your assets pass directly to your spouse, in which case no tax is assessed.

So as you can see, the government is ready to pounce on your mutual fund profits in a number of ways. Your task is to deflect the blow and keep your taxes to a minimum. There are a number of strategies that will help you do this. Some of the more commonly used ones follow.

*Claim all related expenses*   Taxable capital gains are calculated only after all legal expenses have been factored in. This is done in two stages: at the time of your initial purchase and when you sell. When you buy your fund units, your cost for tax purposes will be adjusted to reflect any expenses you incurred in the process, such as sales charges and the transaction fee charged by securities commissions in some provinces. The result is the *adjusted cost base*, the figure you use for determining capital gains or losses down the road.

When you sell, you deduct any related expenses from the gross proceeds of the sale. These would include such things as sales commissions, account closing fees, etc. The difference between the net proceeds you

the fine print

**ADJUSTED COST BASE**

Here's an example of how an adjusted cost base would be calculated:

| | |
|---|---|
| Price paid for fund units | $1,000.00 |
| Sales commission | 50.00 |
| Ontario Securities Commission fee | .50 |
| Adjusted cost base | $1,050.50 |

receive and the adjusted cost base is the amount subject to tax. If your proceeds are less than the adjusted cost base, you have a capital loss, which can be offset against any taxable capital gains you may have resulting from other transactions.

*Have the lower-income spouse do the family investing* If you're a two-income family, have the spouse with the lower income (who presumably is in a lower tax bracket) acquire the investments. This way you'll pay less tax on any distributions or capital gains.

*Don't buy funds at year-end* Many mutual funds only make distributions once a year, around the end of December. This can create a tax trap that many people are unaware of. The problem arises when you buy these funds outside a registered plan just before the distribution date. Income earned over the previous 12 months is then paid out to investors, including you, and the fund's unit value is adjusted downward to reflect this. The effect is that you receive back some of the investment capital you just paid in, and you have to pay tax on it. It's a situation to avoid.

*Set up your registered and non-registered portfolios to minimize taxes* A good rule of thumb is to use your RRSP to hold securities that attract the highest rate of tax. In the case of mutual funds, this would include any fund that's designed to generate interest as the prime source of income. This includes money market funds, bond funds, and mortgage funds. Keep funds that enjoy a tax advantage outside the retirement plan. These include stock funds (dividends and capital gains), dividend income funds (dividends), and real estate funds (rental income). It won't al-

danger zone

## CARELESS ADVISORS

It may be difficult to believe, but some professional investment advisors fail to take taxes into account when constructing portfolios for their clients. I recently saw a case where an investment counsellor had set up a registered and non-registered portfolio for an individual, each of which held exactly the same securities. When the portfolios were rearranged for maximum tax benefit, the savings amounted to almost $2,000 a year.

ways be possible to set up your portfolios in a such a perfect way, but apply this principle whenever it's feasible.

*Invest in funds for your children*
You can reduce the family tax bite by putting some of your mutual fund investments into your children's names, but you must be careful. Any interest or dividends earned in this situation will be attributed back to you for tax purposes. But capital gains won't be; they're considered to belong to the child. So choose the funds with care. Special tip: if the child has any independent income, such as from an after-school job, he or she can use this money to invest in funds (or anything else) without any tax being attributed back to you at all.

*Take advantage of labour-sponsored funds* A new category of mutual funds offers special tax breaks to investors. They're called labour-sponsored venture capital funds and they're becoming increasingly popular among people looking for a tax advantage. The federal government offers a tax credit of 20 percent of the total amount invested in qualifying funds, up to a total credit of $1,000 a year. Several provinces also offer similar credits against provincial taxes. As a result, in many parts of Canada, you can earn up to $2,000 in tax credits from a $5,000 investment. The credit is deducted directly from your tax payable, so you get the benefit of the full amount, not a percentage as in the case of personal tax credits. Units in these funds are eligible for RRSPs, so you can add to your tax break in this way. In fact, a top-bracket Ontario taxpayer would end up paying a net amount of only $340 for $5,000 worth of fund units if they were bought for an RRSP, after all credits and deductions were taken into account. But a word of warning: these funds invest in small, start-up companies. As a result, they're much higher risk than the average mutual fund. And once you buy your units, you're locked in for a period of time (in most cases, at least five years). Ontario residents have the largest number of labour-sponsored funds to choose from that offer both federal and provincial credits. In some provinces (B.C., Quebec, Manitoba) only one provincially sponsored fund qualifies for tax credits from both levels of government.

*trade talk*

**FREE TAX ADVICE**

The University Avenue Funds put out a useful annual booklet on the tax implications of mutual fund investing. You can get a free copy by calling 1-800-465-1812.

Ontario residents have **the largest number of labour-sponsored funds** to choose from that offer both federal and provincial credits.

As you can see, you can use a number of strategies to keep your mutual fund tax bill as low as possible. But the plain fact is that, as with anything else, if you make money from your mutual funds (which is, after all, the only reason to invest in them), you'll have to share at least some of it with Revenue Canada. They wouldn't have it any other way.

# Money market funds are

the safest type of mutual fund investment, but they aren't completely risk free. . . . Historical performance is of little importance in assessing the future potential of an MMF. The direction of short-term interest rates is much more significant. . . . Big funds often offer lower expense ratios, with consequently higher returns. . . .

Canadians have fallen in love with money market funds (MMFs). At the beginning of 1996, we had almost $20 billion invested in this type of mutual fund. That's a lot of money!

What's the attraction? Well, consider this. Bank savings accounts used to be the most popular place to hold spare cash. But then the banks decided, for whatever reason, that they didn't want to encourage this practice anymore. They slashed interest rates on savings accounts to the bone: As we entered 1996, some major banks were actually paying less than 1 percent on basic savings accounts. At the same time, they imposed fees on all kinds of services that used to be free. Bank profits soared, but customers gradually began to realize they should start seeking other alternatives.

An excellent option was available just a counter away—money market funds. They offered a much better yield than savings accounts, and there was no cost attached to them. The average Canadian MMF returned 6.2 percent for the 12 months to November 30, 1995. No bank could offer a savings account that even came close.

## the fine print

**MONEY MARKET FUNDS**

These funds invest in short-term securities, such as government Treasury bills. The unit value is generally maintained at a fixed level ($10 is usual), so there is little risk of loss. They're considered to be the safest type of mutual fund you can buy.

But the attractive yield isn't the only reason for the rapid growth in these funds. Convenience is another big plus. Almost every bank and trust company now has at least one MMF and perhaps as many as three or four available. For example, CIBC has a regular CIBC Money Market Fund, a CIBC Canadian T-Bill Fund (for those looking for an extra measure of security), a CIBC U.S. Dollar Money Market Fund, and a "premium" fund, which offers superior returns to investors with $250,000 or more.

Perhaps the biggest attraction of money market funds is that they are seen as a safe haven for cash, even though they have no deposit insurance protection. Many MMFs use Government of Canada Treasury bills as their core holding, which gives them an image of soundness and stability. This is reinforced by the fact that no Canadian MMF that I'm aware of has ever lost money for its investors.

Many MMFs use **Government of Canada Treasury bills** as their core holding, which gives them an image of soundness and stability.

So no wonder the cash has been pouring in. As of December 1995, MMFs managed by members of the Investment Funds Institute of Canada, the umbrella association of the mutual funds industry, had over 1.2 million accounts, up 50 percent from the previous year. Clearly, money market funds are an idea whose time has come, at least as far as Canadian investors are concerned (Americans discovered their advantages years ago).

However, many people who are putting their cash into money market funds don't fully understand what they're investing in or have unrealistic expectations of these funds. First, it's important to realize that MMFs invest exclusively in short-term securities, which usually have maturities of less than a year. A fund's holdings can range from high-grade T-Bills to short-term commercial notes issued by corporations. The return paid by any given fund will therefore fluctuate on a daily basis. When interest rates are rising and new money can be invested in securities with an ever-higher yield, the total return from your MMF investment will steadily increase. But when interest rates are falling, as they were through the early '90s and again entering 1996, yields will decline as maturing securities have to be rolled over at a lower rate. The result is that the return on your investment steadily drops. For people living on a fixed income who depend on their investments to put bread on the table, this can be a serious problem.

For example, when interest rates were high in 1990, most Canadian dollar money market funds were generating returns in the 12 percent range. *The Globe and Mail*'s "Report on Business" found that the average return for all Canadian-based money market funds during the year was 11.8 percent. This included a few U.S. dollar and international MMFs, which had reduced returns because of lower interest rates outside Canada.

Investors were obviously impressed with such good results from low-risk funds, and the cash kept flowing in. All the while, however, forward-looking financial advisors were warning clients not to become mesmerized by the high MMF yields. Investors were told to lock in high rates for the long term by switching into five-year GICs or to move into bonds or bond funds for a combination of high yields and capital gains as interest rates declined, as they inevitably would. Some people listened. But many more stuck with the MMFs.

What happened? By July 1991, MMF yields had fallen to a range of 8–9 percent, with some as low as 7.25 percent. That was down about four percentage points from 1990. With the economy in trouble and interest rates declining, it appeared a virtual certainty yields would drop further.

They did. By mid-1992, few money market funds were returning more than 6 percent and some were probing 5 percent territory. And the trend was still down. By the beginning of 1994, most MMFs were yielding between 2.5 and 3.5 percent. Yields improved during that year, as rates moved back up. But by late 1995, short-term interest rates were falling again, signalling that MMF yields in 1996 would be heading lower.

This is the underlying danger of money market funds. By leaving your cash in them when interest rates are falling, you'll experience a lower return and miss opportunities to make bigger profits elsewhere. This is not to say money market funds are bad or should not be used. As with all other forms of investing, they should be used intelligently.

There is no longer any reason to hold large amounts of cash in savings accounts. Your money will work harder for you in an MMF.

MMFs have two valuable functions. The first is that they provide a safe haven for your money during periods of financial turmoil, especially when short-term interest rates are high. The second is that they are a substitute for deposit accounts. In fact, as I said at the beginning of this chapter, there is no valid reason for holding large amounts of money in savings accounts anymore, as an increasing number of Canadians have concluded. Even the best of these accounts is unlikely to offer a better return than a money market fund. Obviously, you need to retain a chequing account to handle current cash flow (although some MMFs now offer limited chequing privileges). But any cash you would otherwise keep in a savings account for easy access will work harder for you in a money market fund. And, in most cases, you can withdraw it just as quickly if you need to.

So which MMF should you choose? Since money market funds have taken off, the marketplace has been flooded with new products. There has also been some behind-the-scenes manoeuvring on the part of some mutual fund operators in an effort to gain a competitive edge. This has created confusion among investors looking for the best MMF deal. To help you make the right choice, here are a dozen guidelines to follow:

the fine print

**CURRENT YIELD**

The actual return of a money market fund over the past seven days, projected over one year.

*1. Don't put too much emphasis on comparative rates of return.* The mutual fund industry has been going through a bitter internal conflict over the proper way to report MMF yields, and it's not over yet. As things stand now, fund companies must use current yield in their advertising. However, there's no uniformity in the way this is reported. Some funds do the calculation daily, using a rolling seven-day average; some tumble the numbers only once a week.

Funds are also allowed to promote their effective yield, as long as it is not given greater prominence than the current yield in any ad. The effective yield brings the advantage of compounding into play. It is supposed to indicate what the fund will yield over the next twelve months, based on the current yield and assuming all interest is reinvested and compounded weekly. The Investment Funds Institute of Canada carries out and reports this calculation for its members.

If you check the daily mutual fund reports in the business press, you'll find both yields shown for MMFs.

However, both can be seriously flawed and should not be used as the sole basis for a purchase decision. A fund's current yield can be distorted in a number of ways. For example, some aggressive fund managers loaded up on 364-day Government of Canada Treasury bills in the fall of 1990, when interest rates were still high. As rates dropped over the winter and spring of 1991, they sold some of these longer-term bills, earning capital gains in the process. These gains were reflected in current yields and, by extension, in effective yields. This produced situations in which some funds appeared to be generating returns that were two or three percentage points higher than those of their competitors—a huge differential in an investment area where relative performance is measured in tenths and even hundredths of a percentage point.

Again, when interest rates spiked up during the 1992 referendum campaign, some managers invested large amounts of money (in one case, $100 million) in what's called the overnight market. These rates were unusually high at the time because the Bank of Canada was using them to attempt to restore order to nervous currency markets. These bonus rates showed up in the current yield—the weighted average of book yields of all securities in the portfolio over the previous seven days. Then, even worse, they were compounded by the application of the effective yield formula to produce a theoretical return that a fund would generate if these rates were in force for a full year. Of course, they weren't. As currency markets

**danger zone**

**ASSUMING TOO MUCH**

At the beginning of 1996, some Canadian money market funds were showing effective yields in the 6 percent range. But short-term interest rates were dropping, with yields on three-month Canada T-bills down to 5.5 percent. In those circumstances, a return of close to 6 percent on an MMF in 1996 looked highly unlikely, especially considering that most funds have to pay an annual management fee of 1 percent or more.

settled down, overnight rates dropped to more normal levels. But for a period of time, managers who used this approach looked like they were geniuses, and the result may have been more business from unknowing investors. This kind of activity underlines the importance of not taking high MMF performance numbers at face value.

Also, remember that as interest rates drop, so will the effective yield of MMFs. You should not expect a fund that projects a 4.5 percent effective yield today to actually deliver this rate of return over the next 12 months if interest rates decline during that period. Of course if rates rise, the yield will too. In short, there are no guarantees. In fact, the numbers that are quoted by the funds are not projected yields at all but historical rates of return. They assume everything will remain the same for the next 12 months, which, of course, won't happen. So don't be misled into believing the quoted yields are what you'll actually receive. They aren't!

*2. Ask about special deals.* Another tactic sometimes used by money market funds to attract business is a temporary reduction or suspension of management fees. These deals provide a bonus for investors, because reduced management fees increase your return. However, they also artificially inflate the published yields for such funds. Investors who use yields to help make a purchase decision may be led to believe a particular fund is outperforming its competitors when in reality the edge comes from a temporary lowering of its management fees.

Before making an investment decision, ask whether there are any factors that are temporarily distorting a fund's current yield in comparison with other MMFs. If there are, take this into account in your selection.

*3. Consider the safety factor.* Although MMFs as a group have an excellent record, some are inherently less risky than others. However, expect to pay a price for increased safety.

danger zone

## SMOKE AND MIRRORS

If you scan the monthly mutual fund reports in the business pages looking for low management expense ratios, your eye may be drawn to the Elliott & Page Money Fund. It shows an MER of only 0.21 percent—the lowest in the industry. In fact, no one else even comes close. And the returns look terrific, as well. But hold on. If something seems to good to be true, it probably is. This is certainly the case here. This fund's MER looks so low because it doesn't reflect the full negotiable annual management fee of up to 1 percent that you'll be hit with when you acquire units. In most funds, the management fee is deducted from the assets of the portfolio. But here, you're assessed the fee directly. Since E&P doesn't show the potential maximum effect of the equation when it publishes its results, this fund may look much better than it actually is.

Canadian money market funds are not as tightly regulated as those in the United States in terms of the quality of the securities they may hold. As a result, some funds carry a greater degree of risk than others. During good economic times, this may not seem particularly important, but when business is slow and bankruptcies are a problem, it's worth taking into account.

Funds that invest largely or exclusively in Government of Canada Treasury bills rank highest on the safety scale. They're usually called *T-bill funds*. Other MMFs may hold a higher percentage of commercial short-term paper in their portfolios. The yields on these securities will be higher than on government T-bills, but their safety rating will be lower. You'll have to decide how much safety you're prepared to sacrifice for enhanced returns. Before you make the decision, ask for a copy of the fund's current portfolio and investment philosophy. Review both carefully to see how they fit with your needs.

*4. Ask about average term to maturity.* Yields on MMFs will rise or fall from current levels in the months ahead, depending on the course interest rates take. If rates are expected to drop, your objective should be to invest in a fund that will experience a slower-than-average yield decline. So you want one with a longer average term to maturity. The reverse holds true when rates are rising. In this case, the shorter the term to maturity the better, because the fund will be able to roll over its assets into higher-yielding securities at an earlier date.

*5. Look for no-charge switching.* A money market fund should be regarded as a temporary parking place for cash. You should therefore select a fund that allows you to switch your assets easily, and without cost, to other types of funds, such as bond or equity funds. If you have to pay a fee to switch, it will cut into your yield significantly. And it may inhibit you from making a change that good investment sense would otherwise dictate.

*6. Don't pay any sales or redemption charges.* The difference between the yields of competitive money market funds is usually so small that any load charge or redemption cost will almost always tip the balance in favour of a no-load fund.

Most companies, even those that charge front-or back-end loads on all their other funds, will provide MMFs on a no-load basis. But you may have to negotiate with the salesperson to get a no-load deal. If this doesn't work, contact the mutual fund company directly. If they still want to charge a fee, look elsewhere.

*7. Look closely at the management fees.* The returns on MMFs will be greatly affected by the management fee structure, more so than any other type of mutual fund. This is because these funds usually generate relatively low returns to begin with. After management fees and expenses are deducted, the profit left for investors is small. A management expense ratio of about 1 percent is normal for an MMF. Anything over 1.5 percent is high. Under 0.75 percent is a bargain.

the fine print

## A TALE OF TWO FUNDS

Compare the annual rates of return of these two funds from two major chartered banks for the period ending November 30, 1995. These figures were reported in *The Globe and Mail*. Note how much of the difference can be directly attributed to the management charges. The Green Line fund is offered by Toronto Dominion Bank, the RoyFund by Royal Bank. The Green Line fund's advantage is primarily due to the fact that it is almost 10 times the size of the RoyFund, so it is able to operate more cost-effectively.

| Fund | MER | 1 Year | 2 Years | 3 Years |
|---|---|---|---|---|
| Green Line Canadian Money Market Fund | 0.77% | 6.3% | 5.4% | 5.2% |
| RoyFund Canadian Money Market Fund | 1.22% | 5.9% | 4.8% | 4.6% |

*8. Check the size of the fund.* When it comes to money market funds, small is usually not beautiful. A bigger fund can spread its costs over a larger asset base, making it more efficient and reducing the drain on unitholder returns in percentage terms.

*9. Ask about ease of redemption.* One of the advantages of money market funds is the ability to move cash in and out easily. Inquire about the redemption policy of the fund you're considering. If it's only valued once a week, for example, you may have to wait a few days for your money.

*10. See what "extras" are offered.* The competition between MMFs has led some companies to offer valuable bonuses to get your business. Some funds, for example, now provide limited chequing privileges, which is a common benefit in the U.S. In Canada, both the Industrial Cash Management Fund and the Hodgson Roberton Laing Instant $$ Fund offer this feature. See if the fund you're considering has any such perks and weigh their relative importance to you.

*11. Use MMFs to protect your currency base.* The Canadian dollar has been weak through much of the '90s. In 1991, it was worth over US89¢. Entering 1996, it was trading at close to US74¢. This has led many investors to look for ways to protect their assets from further currency debasement.

Investing in U.S. dollar and international money market funds is one way to do this. At first glance, U.S. dollar MMFs don't look particularly attractive; their average annual compound rate of return for the three-year period ending November 30, 1995, was only about 3.5 percent. But this number is deceiving because U.S. dollar MMFs are the only mutual funds sold in Canada that do not include exchange rate fluctuations in their performance results. If you factor in the Canadian dollar's decline in value during this period—a decline of about 17 percent compared to U.S. currency—you get a very different performance picture.

International MMFs are still new and there were only two to choose from at the beginning of 1996: the Altamira Short-Term Global Income Fund and the Global Strategy Diversified Short-Term Income Fund. They invest in short-term securities denominated in a variety of currencies, which makes them a good choice at times when both the U.S. and Canadian dollar are under pressure.

danger zone

**AN IMPORTANT DISTINCTION**

Unlike all other money market funds, international MMFs do not attempt to maintain a fixed unit value. The price will fluctuate, depending on the market value of the securities in the portfolio. So these funds carry a higher measure of risk than other MMFs and can suffer losses as a result. For example, the Altamira Short-Term Global Income Fund was down 0.8 percent in value for the 12 months to November 30, 1995.

*12. Don't assume you can't lose money.* The net asset value of Canadian MMFs is supposedly fixed, usually at $10. In the case of all other types of mutual funds, the NAV will fluctuate depending on the market value of the securities in the portfolio. This gives MMFs a unique advantage. You know (or think you know) that if you put in $100, you'll get this amount back plus interest when the time comes to cash in. Sort of like a more flexible version of a GIC.

Unfortunately, a potential trap exists for unwary investors. The value of the securities in an MMF portfolio may indeed fluctuate, even if the fund invests exclusively in Treasury bills. For example, when interest rates soared in September 1992 in response to heavy pressure on the Canadian dollar arising from the referendum campaign on the Charlottetown Accord, the value of all fixed income securities, including T-bills and short-term commercial notes, took a hit. As a result, some funds saw a sudden drop in the value of their portfolio. If money market funds were valued in the same way as all other mutual funds, this would have been reflected in a lower unit value. But since their value is fixed (albeit artificially) managers had to find another way to make up the shortfall. At least one company, Elliott & Page, did this by suspending interest payments for a month. So investors in their money market fund received no return during this time. The units held their value. But they didn't earn any money.

The shorter the term to maturity of an MMF portfolio, the less the risk. This is because the less time remaining to a security's redemption, the less vulnerable it is to interest rate fluctuations. But if wild movements in rates return, we could see a situation sometime in the future when a money market fund is forced to abandon the fixed rate standard and pass on losses to investors in the form of a lower unit value. So although these funds are low risk, they are not entirely risk free.

While we're on the subject of loss potential, remember that MMFs are *not* covered by deposit insurance, even if they're purchased at a financial institution that's a CDIC member. The risk of serious loss is very low, but it cannot be dismissed entirely.

One final word of warning. Some money market funds are being used to attract investors, with the idea of switching them into other funds later. Salespeople may be offered attractive commissions to switch buyers into other funds and buyers will sometimes be charged a fee for this.

Before you invest, look at all the funds in the family of the MMF you're considering. See how they measure up compared to the competition and decide whether you would consider investing in them on their own merits. If they don't look attractive, don't give the company your MMF business, especially if you're making the investment within a registered plan, such as an RRSP. You'll only create complications for yourself when the time comes to move on.

# Fixed income funds should

be a part of every portfolio, but there are different types
of funds for different needs. . . . There are two types of
international bond funds, one of which is fully eligible for
RRSPs. . . . Bond funds can generate some handsome
capital gains, if used correctly. . . .

There's a tendency among younger people to think that fixed income
funds are for their parents. Dull funds for old folks, if you like.
There's no action in bond funds, no
excitement in mortgage funds or
dividend funds. They may be okay
some day when retirement income
is needed. But not now. Please!

Well, I have news for you. Yes, it's
true that fixed income funds are useful for generating retirement income.
However, there's much more to
them than that. In fact, certain fixed
income funds offer significant capital gains potential—with all the con-
comitant risks. Every mutual funds
portfolio should contain some fixed
income funds. But which type of funds, and in what proportion, will
depend on your investment goals and on general economic conditions.

Before we get into the strategies of fixed income investing, let's look
at the different types of funds that are available.

the fine print

**FIXED INCOME
FUNDS**

These mutual funds specialize
in securities that offer a
specified rate of return for a
defined term of a year or more.
These include regular bonds,
convertible bonds, preferred
shares, mortgages, and
mortgage-backed securities.

## CANADIAN BOND FUNDS

These invest in bonds and debentures issued by Canadian governments and corporations. The portfolio is usually a mix of short- and longer- term bonds; the weighting is adjusted by the manager depending on the prospects for interest rates and the bond market.

inside info

**PSEUDO-WINNERS**

International bonds funds are a relatively new phenomenon in Canada, so no clear patterns have yet been established as to which type performs better. However, it's interesting to note that over the three-year period to November 30, 1995, the two top spots went to pseudo-international funds that are fully RRSP eligible. Dynamic Global Bond Fund topped the list with an average annual return of 12 percent over this period. Runner-up was the Royal Trust International Bond Fund, at 10.6 percent a year.

## INTERNATIONAL BOND FUNDS

These funds invest in bonds and debentures that are denominated in currencies other than the Canadian dollar. There are two types of international funds:

Pure international funds   These invest in securities issued by foreign governments and corporations. They are classified as foreign content for RRSP purposes.

Pseudo-international funds   These funds invest in securities issued by Canadian entities that are denominated in foreign currencies. The federal and provincial governments routinely issue bonds in U.S. dollars, Japanese yen, German marks, etc., as a means of encouraging foreign investors to assume a portion of our deficit financing. Because the bonds are Canadian in origin, they count as domestic content for RRSPs. As well, the federal Finance Department has declared that bonds issued by certain international financial institutions, such as the World Bank, qualify as Canadian content. These funds invest in a mix of all these securities, retaining full RRSP eligibility in the process.

Short-term bond funds are **defensive funds** for people who want to minimize risk but obtain a better return than money market funds normally offer.

## SHORT-TERM BOND FUNDS

These funds first appeared in the mid-'90s, mainly in response to the crash of the bond market in early 1994. They're a cross between a regular bond fund and a money market fund. The managers invest in securities with a maximum term of three or five years (each fund sets its own policy). The idea is to reduce risk by keeping the term short (the shorter the term of a bond, the less the impact of interest rate movements on its price). These are defensive funds for people who want to keep risk to a minimum but obtain a better return than money market funds normally offer. Typically, they will drop less in value than a regular bond fund in bad times, but they won't produce gains of the same magnitude when markets are good.

## HIGH-YIELD BOND FUNDS

These funds seek out bonds that pay higher-than-normal rates of interest, with the goal of producing better returns than an ordinary bond fund can provide. In the U.S., they're known as junk bond funds, because

trade talk

**COMPARING COUSINS**

Here are some examples of how regular bond funds and short-term bond funds in the same family performed over the 12-month period to November 30, 1995. This was a strong period for bond markets, so you'd expect the regular funds to do better, which is exactly what happened.

| Fund | Return |
|---|---|
| Altamira Bond Fund | 28.5% |
| Altamira Short-Term Government Bond Fund | 15.0% |
| Green Line Canadian Bond Fund | 20.1% |
| Green Line Short-Term Income Fund | 10.4% |
| Phillips, Hager & North Bond Fund 1 | 9.5% |
| Phillips, Hager & North Short-Term Bond & Mortgage Fund | 14.4% |
| Scotia Excelsior Income Fund | 20.2% |
| Scotia Excelsior Defensive Income Fund | 13.4% |

many of the securities in which they invest are higher risk. The managers of these funds look for bonds issued by companies with low credit ratings but that appear to be in a good enough financial position to maintain their interest payments. There are only a few of these funds in Canada.

### MORTGAGE FUNDS

For the most part, these funds invest in residential first mortgages. However, a few also hold commercial mortgages. After money market funds, mortgage funds are considered to be the lowest-risk type of mutual fund you can buy. Defaults by mortgage holders are rare in Canada, and the relatively short term of these funds makes them less vulnerable to price changes due to interest rate fluctuations. A few fund companies even go so far as to guarantee that any defaulting mortgages will be repurchased from the fund with no penalty to unitholders (Bank of Montreal does this for the First Canadian Mortgage Fund).

### trade talk

**STRONG START**

One good example of a Canadian high-yield bond fund is the Trimark Advantage Bond Fund. Launched in December 1994, it got off to a strong start with a gain of 21.4 percent in its first year.

### MORTGAGE-BACKED FUNDS

These are a variation on regular mortgage funds. They invest a significant portion of their portfolio in mortgage-backed securities, which are guaranteed for both principal and interest by Canada Mortgage and Housing Corporation (so, in essence, by the Government of Canada). There are no pure mortgage-backed funds in Canada, but the Industrial Mortgage Securities Fund invests at least half its portfolio in these issues.

### DIVIDEND INCOME FUNDS

I include these funds in this chapter because there's no other logical place for them. However, I do so reluctantly since there is no consistency in the offerings from different fund groups. A pure dividend income fund invests almost exclusively in preferred shares and high-yielding common stocks, such as banks and utilities. The objective is to maximize dividend income, which is taxed at a lower rate than interest because of the application of the dividend tax credit. However, several so-called dividend funds have portfolios that don't truly reflect this philosophy. They may hold bonds, common stocks that pay little or no dividend, or even foreign securities that don't qualify for the dividend tax credit at all. If tax-advantaged income is your main objective, be very selective.

inside info

**GOOD DIVIDEND FUNDS**

Some of the funds that come closest to meeting my definition of a true dividend income fund because of their focus on preferred shares and high-yielding common stocks are the Dynamic Dividend Fund, the Guardian Monthly Dividend Fund, the Laurentian Dividend Fund, and the Scotia Excelsior Dividend Fund.

INCOME FUNDS

These are something of a hybrid. The managers may invest in just about anything from the fixed income securities list, from long-term bonds to mortgage-backed securities. Before putting any money into one of these funds, find out where the portfolio emphasis lies and decide if it's consistent with what you're trying to achieve.

So that's the rather lengthy list of fixed income options. As you can see, there's much to choose from, and not all the fund types will be right for everyone. The next step is to consider some of the most common fixed income investing

If you're thinking of investing in a fixed income fund, remember that interest rates and bond prices move in opposite directions. When interest rates decline, bond prices rise, and vice-versa.

strategies and decide which of these funds best suits your specific goals.

Before we do this, however, there's a basic principle of investing that must be taken into account whenever you're considering a fixed income fund. It's this: *Interest rates and bond prices move in opposite directions.* Technically, this is called an inverse relationship. When interest rates decline, bond prices rise, and vice-versa. It seems very elementary, but many people aren't aware of this principle and don't understand how to use it to their advantage.

### the fine print

### HOW IT WORKS

Many people have trouble understanding why if interest rates go up, a bond's price goes down. Let's reduce it to simple terms. Suppose you own a 10-year Government of Canada bond that pays 7 percent interest a year. This is a fixed rate (called the coupon rate), and it doesn't change. Now rates rise and new Canada 10-year issues pay 8 percent. Why would anyone pay full price for your bond, with its 7 percent coupon? The answer is they wouldn't—unless you reduced the asking price of the bond to compensate them for the lower return.

Although I've made reference to bond prices in stating the principle, it applies to all fixed income securities, including mortgages and preferred shares. However, it's important to note that the degree of impact on the price of any given security will be directly affected by its term to maturity. The longer the time remaining until maturity, the more the price will be moved by a rise or fall in interest rates.

Look at it this way. Suppose you have two bonds, each of which pays 8 percent annual interest. One matures next year; the other has 20 years to run. Interest rates drop and new issues are paying only 6 percent. This makes your bonds, with their higher coupon rate, more attractive to investors. But the bond with one year to maturity only pays the premium rate for a limited time. The other one continues to generate above-average income for two decades. It's not hard to figure out which one is worth more to other investors.

Keeping all this in mind, let's look now at some fixed income fund strategies.

*The compound interest approach* This is the most common use for fixed income funds. The idea is to use the steady returns provided by these funds over time to maximize the effect of compound interest in your portfolio. You can achieve the same result with GICs, of course, but a well-selected group of fixed income funds will usually provide a better return over time. Mortgage funds and conservatively managed bond funds work most effectively. This strategy works best inside a registered plan, such as an RRSP, where tax sheltering will maximize the return.

*The capital gains gambit* Many new fund investors don't realize that bond funds can produce some very healthy capital gains. This strategy seeks to take advantage of the interest rate/bond price relationship to generate this type of profit. The idea is to load up on bond funds during periods when interest rates are high and expected to fall. As rates move down, bond prices will react and fund unit values will rise. Holdings are reduced when rates appear to be bottoming out in order to lock in the profits. Experienced investors who use this strategy seek out bond funds where the managers have overweighted their portfolios with long-term issues—the ones that will do best in

## the fine print

### THE DIVIDEND TAX CREDIT

The dividend tax credit is intended to reduce the effect of double taxation by recognizing that corporate dividends are distributed to shareholders out of after-tax profits. This means a company has already paid tax once on the earnings. In theory, therefore, dividends should then be received tax free, but governments aren't that generous. The dividend tax credit is a compromise measure. To calculate the credit to which you're entitled, you must first "gross up" the actual dividend you receive by multiplying the amount by 125 percent. You then multiply this number by 13.33 percent. The amount of the credit is deducted directly from your federal tax payable. Note that the dividend tax credit will only apply to dividends your fund receives from taxable Canadian corporations. Dividends from foreign companies aren't eligible.

a falling interest rate environment. Obviously, this is a higher risk strategy—if you guess wrong and rates rise, you'll be faced with some heavy losses in your portfolio. If this happens, don't panic and sell. Rates will inevitably come back down. They always do.

*The steady income plan*   One of the strengths of fixed income funds is that they generate a regular income for investors. This makes them especially useful for people who have reached retirement age and are planning to live on their investment income. If this is how you want to use your fixed income portfolio, find out how often the funds you're considering make distributions. Some people prefer funds that offer monthly payments, to ensure a regular cash flow. Others are content with quarterly distributions. If a fund's distributions are less frequent (only once or twice a year), the fund won't be suitable for this purpose.

*The tax-advantaged income tactic* Some fixed income funds can be used to generate tax-advantaged income. This simply means your payments will be taxed at a lower than normal rate. Dividend income funds are the best choice here because most (but not necessarily all) of the money they distribute to unitholders qualifies for the dividend tax credit. To take maximum advantage of this, make sure you keep your fund units outside a registered plan, choose a fund that invests mainly in preferred shares and high yielding common stocks, and make sure distributions take place at least quarterly.

*The capital protection strategy* If safety is a prime concern, fixed income funds can be used effectively to protect your capital from loss. In this case, you'll want to focus mainly on fixed income funds with the lowest risk. Mortgage funds, short-term bond funds, and funds based on mortgage-backed securities are most suitable for this type of portfolio.

*The currency hedge* Finally, fixed income funds can be used to give your mutual fund portfolio some protection against possible future declines in the value of the Canadian dollar. Unfortunately, our currency has a history of being highly volatile. In the past decade, one Canuck buck has been worth as much as US89¢ and as little as US69¢. This represents a swing in value of almost 30 percent, which is far too great for the comfort of any conservative investor. By adding international bond funds denominated in some of the world's strongest currencies to your portfolio, you can reduce this risk somewhat. But be careful. If the Canadian dollar should rise sharply in value against other currencies, it will

inside info

**SAFETY FIRST!**

Here's how fixed income funds rank on a safety scale, moving from least risk to highest risk. A pure mortgage-backed fund would rate as number one for safety, but there are none available at the time of writing. The Industrial Mortgage Securities Fund, for example, can hold up to 30 percent of its portfolio in stocks, thereby increasing the risk factor. Thus the mortgage-backed funds rate farther down the scale. Remember, this is only a generalization. The style of individual portfolio managers will play a major role in the risk level of any fund.

| | |
|---|---|
| Mortgage funds | Low risk |
| Short-term bond funds | |
| Mortgage-backed funds | |
| Income funds | |
| Canadian bond funds | Medium risk |
| International bond funds | |
| Dividend income funds | |
| High-yield bond funds | Higher risk |

have a negative effect on the value of these funds. Currency volatility cuts both ways. I suggest using international bond funds as a hedge only during periods when our dollar is weak.

Every mutual fund portfolio should hold some fixed income funds as part of the total asset mix. As a general rule, not less than 25 percent of your holdings should be in these funds, with a maximum of 75 percent for older people who are looking mainly for steady income and safety.

I recommend that younger people who are just getting into fund investing begin with more conservative fixed income funds. Psychology plays a big role in investing success; if you start with a high-risk fund and lose money, you could be put off fund investing for life. It's better to choose a low-risk fund at the outset. As it starts to show gains, your confidence level will increase and you can move on to other areas.

# Equity funds offer the

greatest potential for large gains in the mutual fund world. However, they can lose money too. . . . Sector funds are relatively new to Canada, but some have had spectacular results. . . . Minimize your equity fund risk by diversifying internationally and carefully monitoring the total percentage of stock funds in your portfolio. . . .

We've saved the best for last. Money market and fixed income funds are valuable additions to any mutual fund portfolio, but the real action is in equity funds. This is where you can score the biggest gains, or suffer the worst losses if you choose badly and the market moves against you. This is why you need to exercise extreme care when selecting a fund. Make sure you know exactly what you're buying and the risks involved. That's what this chapter is about.

There is a broad range of equity funds from which to choose. An equity fund is one that invests primarily in stocks traded on recognized exchanges. They fall into several categories, some of which may overlap. Here's a rundown of the key ones. As you go through it, keep in mind that a single fund may fit into more than one category—for example, an international fund that specializes in small cap stocks.

## SINGLE-COUNTRY FUNDS

These invest primarily, although not necessarily entirely, in shares from a single country. Canadian equity funds, by far the most common type of stock fund offered in this country, fall into this group. U.S. equity

inside info

## ADDING FOREIGN CONTENT

Many Canadian equity funds take advantage of the government's foreign content rules to hold up to 20 percent of their portfolio in international equities. These holdings do not count against your personal foreign content limit if your fund units are in an RRSP or other registered plan. So if you want to increase the foreign holdings in a retirement plan, choose Canadian funds that make maximum use of this provision. The monthly mutual fund survey published by *The Financial Post* is an excellent source for this information.

funds also fit here, and there are about 100 of them available to Canadian investors. There are also about half-a-dozen Japan funds, a couple of Germany funds, an India Fund, and one Korea fund. As well, there are a few so-called China funds, but none are true single-country funds because most of the shares they hold are based in Hong Kong or other Asian countries. No other single-country funds are offered directly here, although Canadian investors can buy a wide range of closed-end single country funds that trade on the New York Stock Exchange.

### REGIONAL FUNDS

These invest in shares of companies located within a geographic region. Included in this group are European funds, Far East funds, North American funds, and Latin American funds. Usually, the manager of a regional fund has the freedom to acquire stocks from any country in the designated area for his portfolio. But sometimes restrictions apply. For example, several Far East funds specifically exclude Japanese stocks. The reason usually given is that Japan is a developed country, while the other Far East markets are not. This creates conflicts in the fund's investment approach. Actually, I suspect the exclusion has more to do with marketing: many fund companies offer both a Far East fund and a Japan fund and want to maintain a clear distinction between the two. The latest phenomenon in regional funds is the Americas fund. This type of fund offers a portfolio that combines U.S. stocks (for stability) with shares from Latin American countries (for greater growth potential). It's a hybrid designed to appeal to investors who would like some exposure to Latin America but don't want the risks associated with a pure Latin fund.

## INTERNATIONAL FUNDS

For the managers of these funds, the world is their oyster. They have the freedom to invest wherever they want for the most part and to stay away completely from countries they think are overpriced or are potential trouble spots. As a result, a well-managed international fund is the lowest-risk type of equity fund you can buy. But you need to be aware of certain fine points. For example, there is a technical distinction between the terms *international fund* and *global fund*. An international fund will not invest in its home country, whereas a global fund will. You may also find restrictions in the investment policies of different funds. The Templeton organization offers a good illustration; the Templeton Growth Fund may invest anywhere in the world, whereas the Templeton International Stock Fund excludes North American shares from its portfolio.

trade talk

**INDIA SETBACK**

The 20/20 fund group launched Canada's first India fund in late 1994. It was a disaster in its first year, losing almost half its initial value. This is an extreme example of the level of risk you can encounter in single-country funds.

## LARGE CAP FUNDS

These funds invest mainly in the shares of large corporations. The theory is that these blue chip stocks are more stable and so this type of fund represents less risk to an investor. This may be true to a degree, but the reality is that if the market goes into a dive, these stocks will, too.

## SMALL CAP FUNDS

At the other end of the spectrum, these funds focus on shares in smaller companies that are deemed to have above-

the fine print

**EMERGING MARKETS FUNDS**

Emerging markets funds are a sub-group of international funds. They focus on developing economies throughout the world, seeking to benefit from their higher growth potential. These funds have proven to be extremely volatile, with big swings in both directions. They're only for investors who are prepared to accept above-average risk.

average growth potential. The definition of a small cap stock differs from one country to another, so the portfolio make-up can look quite different from one fund to another. Canadian investors may select from a wide range of small cap stocks, some of which concentrate on this country, some of which invest mainly in U.S. companies, and some of which are international in scope. These funds are generally regarded as higher risk than those that specialize in large cap issues, but the rewards can be attractive. For example, *The Globe and Mail* reported an average return of 19.2 percent for the year ending November 30, 1995, for the funds in its Canadian Small-to-Mid-Cap Category. The average return for other Canadian stock funds during this period was 13.6 percent.

The best performing Canadian small cap fund over the five-year period to November 30, 1995, was the Marathon Equity Fund. It generated an average annual return of 31.5 percent during this period.

VENTURE CAPITAL FUNDS

These funds invest primarily in young companies that are not publicly listed on any stock exchange. They may be start-up operations or companies in need of capital to expand their business. This type of fund is extremely high risk, and investors can face heavy losses. (The Integrated Growth Fund reported a drop of 20.3 percent in unit value for the year ending November 30, 1995.) As a result, most activity is centred in the labour-sponsored funds, which offer significant tax breaks as an inducement to invest.

## SECTOR FUNDS

These funds invest in a specific area of the economy. For many years, the only sector funds available in Canada were in the natural resource and precious metals sectors. But this changed in the early '90s with the launch of several sector funds in such fields as health care, telecommunications, infrastructure, and technology. Some of these funds have done extremely well. In fact, three of the top-performing mutual funds of 1995 were sector funds: the Admax Global Health Sciences Fund (+66.3 percent), the Royal Precious Metals Fund (+63.8 percent), and the Green Line Science and Technology Fund (+51.1 percent). But don't get too carried away by these numbers. In the U.S., where sector funds are much more common, experience indicates that such funds tend to be of the boom or bust variety. When the particular sector is hot, as technology stocks were in 1995, the fund will do well. When the sector goes out of favour, unit values will fall.

inside info

**TIPS AND HIPS**

A low-cost alternative to index funds are the TIPS and HIPS, which trade on the Toronto Stock Exchange. TIPS are shares in a basket of the funds represented by the TSE 35 Index, a blue chip index. HIPS are proxies for the TSE 100, which reflects Canada's 100 largest public companies. You can buy either through a broker. You'll pay a sales commission, but there's no annual management fee, so your return will more closely mirror what the index itself does.

## The Admax Global Health Sciences Fund was the top performer in Canada in 1995.

## INDEX FUNDS

These are passive funds, designed to track the performance of a specific stock index, such as the TSE 300. They're designed for investors who want some exposure to

## trade talk

### NOT ALWAYS WHAT IT SEEMS

The 20/20 Dividend Fund is an example of a so-called dividend income fund that's really something else. Its portfolio is heavily weighted to Canadian blue chip common stocks, some of which pay relatively low dividends. Manager Gord MacDougall also makes maximum use of the 20 percent foreign content allowance, something no pure dividend fund would do since non-Canadian securities don't qualify for the dividend tax credit. So this is really a large cap equity fund and a pretty good one at that. It's unfortunate that the name is likely to confuse investors.

the stock market but don't want to take much risk. Their track record in Canada is mediocre at best.

### DIVIDEND INCOME FUNDS

I've included these again here because some dividend funds are really that in name only. Their portfolio composition actually makes them something else: balanced funds in some cases, large cap funds in others. You'll have to look closely at the securities in the portfolio to determine where the specific fund fits.

At the beginning of 1996, more than 600 equity funds of various types were available to Canadian investors. So the selection process can be difficult, unless you have a sound strategy and you stick to it. Here are some guidelines for choosing winning equity funds, which may help you through the jungle.

Control your risk   Since equity funds represent the highest risk element in any mutual fund portfolio, it's essential to manage this risk effectively. This can be done in several ways.

1. Decide on an acceptable percentage of equity fund holdings. Conservative investors can reduce their risk in the equity area by limiting these funds to 25–30 percent of the total portfolio. (Of course, you can eliminate them entirely, but in doing so you lose all growth potential.) More aggressive investors may want to have their entire portfolio in equity funds, although I would not rec-

ommend this approach. The general rule is the greater the total percentage of equity funds you own, the higher the risk factor in your mutual fund portfolio.

2. Select fund types that best fit your philosophy. You can limit your equity fund risk by concentrating on index funds and large cap funds. Both will experience losses when markets drop, but they're likely to be less severe than with other types of funds. The highest-risk categories of equity funds will be small cap, venture capital, emerging markets and sector funds.

3. Diversify geographically. If you choose only equity funds that focus on a single market (e.g., Canada), your portfolio will be more vulnerable (and therefore higher risk) than if it's well diversified internationally. Adding some broadly based global funds to your mix will enhance stability.

Invest in quality  There are countless equity funds, but only a few have demonstrated the rare combination of top-quality management and first-rate long-term performance. These funds may not always hold their pre-eminent positions, of course, but history indicates that they'll stay at or near the top for at least a decade.

Use special caution in RRSPs  It's all right to include equity funds in your RRSP, if this is the only investment portfolio you have. If you have enough investment money to build a non-registered portfolio as well, keep the equity funds outside the retirement plan. This reduces the RRSP risk and allows you to get the full benefit of the tax advantages associated with equity funds—the dividend tax credit and a reduced tax rate on capital gains.

If you buy equity funds for your RRSP, stick with the

more conservative types. Don't speculate with your retirement savings. Small cap funds, for example, really aren't appropriate for RRSPs because of the higher risk involved.

Spread your money around   Don't invest all the cash you've earmarked for equity funds in a single fund or even with a single company, no matter how good its reputation. Overconcentration can lead to trouble. In the 1980s, for example, the Industrial funds of Mackenzie Financial were the darlings of the industry. Investors were attracted by their good returns and brokers loved to sell them because of the excellent commissions and special incentives they offered. But in the early '90s, they ran into trouble when the managers overcommitted all the equity portfolios to resource stocks too early in the cycle. The funds languished and investors complained bitterly. Mackenzie learned an important lesson as a result; the company now offers three distinct fund groups, each with its own separate managerial team. I suggest you spread your equity fund investments among three good fund companies or, at least, three different fund groups, such as those offered by Mackenzie.

One last comment about equity funds. Don't rush to put a lot of money in them after an exceptionally good year. Chances are that after a big run, the markets will change. Many people decided to get into equity funds for the first time following the spectacular success they enjoyed in 1993, when some funds more than doubled in value and the average Canadian stock fund was up more than 30 percent. These investors then watched in dismay as stock markets in most parts of the world hit rough water in 1994 and fund unit values fell. Some people panicked and sold out—just in time to miss the market rebound in 1995, which more than recouped any losses in most cases.

The best approach to equity funds is to make careful choices and take a long-range view. If the fund is well managed, it will enjoy some very good years along the way and you'll profit accordingly.

# Mutual funds are the best

financial vehicle ever created for small investors. . . .
Don't get careless with your fund investing. You could
end up being burned. . . . The mutual fund world is
constantly changing, so stay current. . . .

If you've read this far, and didn't just skip ahead to read the last chapter first, you should now have a pretty firm grasp of the principles of good mutual fund investing. I wish I could say that this guarantees you'll make money in mutual funds. Unfortunately, I can't—there are no sure things in this world. What I can say with confidence is that what you've learned in this book will greatly improve your odds of success, and will reduce significantly your chances of experiencing any major losses.

But you must not get careless. The financial world is very unforgiving to those who become too nonchalant or, worse, too greedy. The further you get into mutual fund investing, the greater the temptation will be to take more chances, to move away from your objectives, to go for the big score. It's natural, and it's dangerous. If you want to invest this way, put aside a little money and speculate in penny mines on the Vancouver Stock Exchange. Or, as one of my brokers advises me, "Go to Vegas. At least you'll have fun while you're losing."

Most mutual funds are not intended to be used as fast-buck vehicles. Rather, they're managed for a combination of long-term profits and reasonable risk, and this should be the approach you bring to them.

There has never been a financial tool better suited to small investors than the mutual fund. You can participate with just a few hundred dollars yet, properly handled, funds can be the foundation for substantial future wealth.

However, they can also be misused in a number of ways. Speculation, leveraging, and panic selling can all result in serious losses, from which it can take years to recover. I don't want to suggest that investing in mutual funds is like playing with fire, but in some ways the analogy isn't inappropriate. Like fire, mutual funds can be a tremendously valuable tool. If you misuse them, though, you can get burned.

So treat them with respect. And remember that even though you've finished reading this book, you haven't come to the end of the learning process. In fact, you've only just begun. The mutual fund world is constantly changing and evolving. New funds appear almost every week, managers switch companies, sales practices evolve, fund groups merge, tax laws are altered—it never ends.

So stay on top of what's happening. Read the business pages, review the monthly fund surveys, check out annual mutual fund guides, subscribe to a newsletter. The more informed you are, the greater your chances of success.

And be realistic in your expectations. A mutual fund portfolio that returns 10–12 percent a year on average over an extended period is producing excellent results. If you can achieve this level of performance, you've done very well. If you do better than this, terrific!

I wish you good luck, and may all your fund choices be the right ones.

# INDEX

The text of this book is set in Caslon 540. This electronic version of the typeface was designed in 1990 by Carol Trombly. The original cut, with its lovely classical forms, was created in 1725 by William Caslon, an english engraver.

It was the American Type Foundry that shortened the descenders of Caslon for advertising printing and named their variation Caslon 540.

Today Caslon still stands as one of history's most important and widely used typefaces.

The sans serif typeface used on the cover and inside of the book is Interstate. Interstate is based on the signage alphabets of the United States Federal Highway Administration. Tobias Frere–Jones designed Interstate in 1993 for the Font Bureau in Boston, Massachusetts.

ACQUISITIONS EDITOR: SARA BORINS
PRODUCTION EDITOR: KELLY DICKSON
COPY EDITOR: DEBORAH VIETS
PRODUCTION COORDINATOR: JULIE PRESTON
ART DIRECTOR: KYLE GELL
PAGE LAYOUT: MICHAEL KELLEY
DESIGN: CONCRETE DESIGN COMMUNICATIONS INC.

PRINTED IN CANADA